Praise for *I*

"What C-level executives read to ke decisions. Timeless classics for indispensable knowledge." - Richard Costello, Manager of Corporate Marketing Communication, General Electric

"Want to know what the real leaders are thinking about now? It's in here." - Carl Ledbetter, SVP & CTO, Novell, Inc.

"Priceless wisdom from experts at applying technology in support of business objectives." - Frank Campagnoni, CTO, GE Global Exchange Services

"Unique insights into the way the experts think and the lessons they've learned from experience." - MT Rainey, Co-CEO, Young & Rubicam/Rainey Kelly Campbell Roalfe

"A must-read for anyone in the industry." - Dr. Chuck Lucier, Chief Growth Officer, Booz-Allen & Hamilton

"Unlike any other business books, *Inside the Minds* captures the essence, the deep-down thinking processes, of people who make things happen." - Martin Cooper, CEO, Arraycomm

"A must-read for those who manage at the intersection of business and technology." - Frank Roney, General Manager, IBM

"A great way to see across the changing marketing landscape at a time of significant innovation." - David Kenny, Chairman and CEO, Digitas

"An incredible resource of information to help you develop outside the box..." - Rich Jernstedt, CEO, Golin/Harris International

"A snapshot of everything you need to know..." - Larry Weber, Founder, Weber Shandwick

"Great information for both novices and experts." - Patrick Ennis, Partner, ARCH Venture Partners

"The only useful way to get so many good minds speaking on a complex topic." - Scott Bradner, Senior Technical Consultant, Harvard University

"Must-have information for business executives." - Alex Wilmerding, Principal, Boston Capital Ventures

www.Aspatore.com

Aspatore Books is the largest and most exclusive publisher of C-level executives (CEO, CFO, CTO, CMO, partner) from the world's most respected companies and law firms. Aspatore annually publishes a select group of C-level executives from the Global 1,000, top 250 law firms (partners and chairs), and other leading companies of all sizes. C-Level Business Intelligence™, as conceptualized and developed by Aspatore Books, provides professionals of all levels with proven business intelligence from industry insiders—direct and unfiltered insight from those who know it best—as opposed to third-party accounts offered by unknown authors and analysts. Aspatore Books is committed to publishing an innovative line of business and legal books, those which lay forth principles and offer insights that when employed, can have a direct financial impact on the reader's business objectives, whatever they may be. In essence, Aspatore publishes critical tools—need-to-read as opposed to nice-to-read books—for all business professionals.

Inside the Minds

The critically acclaimed *Inside the Minds* series provides readers of all levels with proven business intelligence from C-level executives (CEO, CFO, CTO, CMO, partner) from the world's most respected companies. Each chapter is comparable to a white paper or essay and is a future-oriented look at where an industry/profession/topic is heading and the most important issues for future success. Each author has been carefully chosen through an exhaustive selection process by the *Inside the Minds* editorial board to write a chapter for this book. *Inside the Minds* was conceived in order to give readers actual insights into the leading minds of business executives worldwide. Because so few books or other publications are actually written by executives in industry, *Inside the Minds* presents an unprecedented look at various industries and professions never before available.

INSIDE THE MINDS

The Role of a CTO/CIO

Leading Technology Executives on Setting Goals,
Building a Strong Team, and Adding Value to a Company

Mat #40687188

BOOK & ARTICLE IDEA SUBMISSIONS

If you are a C-Level executive, senior lawyer, or venture capitalist interested in submitting a book or article idea to the Aspatore editorial board for review, please email AspatoreAuthors@thomson.com. Aspatore is especially looking for highly specific ideas that would have a direct financial impact on behalf of a reader. Completed publications can range from 2 to 2,000 pages. Include your book/article idea, biography, and any additional pertinent information.

©2005 Thomson/Aspatore
All rights reserved. Printed in the United States of America.

No part of this publication may be reproduced or distributed in any form or by any means, or stored in a database or retrieval system, except as permitted under Sections 107 or 108 of the U.S. Copyright Act, without prior written permission of the publisher. This book is printed on acid free paper.

Material in this book is for educational purposes only. This book is sold with the understanding that neither any of the authors or the publisher is engaged in rendering legal, accounting, investment, or any other professional service. Neither the publisher nor the authors assume any liability for any errors or omissions or for how this book or its contents are used or interpreted or for any consequences resulting directly or indirectly from the use of this book. For legal advice or any other, please consult your personal lawyer or the appropriate professional.

The views expressed by the individuals in this book (or the individuals on the cover) do not necessarily reflect the views shared by the companies they are employed by (or the companies mentioned in this book). The employment status and affiliations of authors with the companies referenced are subject to change.

Aspatore books may be purchased for educational, business, or sales promotional use. For information, please email AspatoreStore@thomson.com.

ISBN 1-59622-321-9
Library of Congress Control Number: 2005934406

For corrections, updates, comments or any other inquiries please email AspatoreEditorial@thomson.com.

First Printing, 2005
10 9 8 7 6 5 4 3 2 1

The Role of a CTO/CIO

*Leading Technology Executives on Setting Goals,
Building a Strong Team, and Adding Value to a Company*

CONTENTS

Setting and Reaching Goals as a Technology Leader

Michael S. Irizarry

Executive Vice President, Engineering
and Chief Technology Officer
U.S. Cellular

The Goals and Responsibilities of a CTO

The primary goal of a chief technology officer (CTO) is to add shareholder value and improve the bottom line profitability of the company. In order to do so, a company must provide a superior network product with the best customer service, which then increases customer loyalty and satisfaction. Within the wireless communications industry, the importance of the customer has become prominent. In the past, as much attention was not placed on the customer because one or two competitors were in the market. In many wireless markets today, there are five or six competitors, and as a result, the way for a company to differentiate itself is to provide a superior customer experience. As a result, the customers remain with the company and enhance its reputation in order to obtain new customers and steal them from competition. Through a series of metrics that are reviewed on a regular basis, a company should benchmark its network and network product with its competitors. Every quarter, a company should measure its systems against the competition, identify the issues, and then take corrective action. By ensuring that customers are provided with the best service and with the best system, a company can improve shareholder value and the bottom line profitability of the company.

In addition, a CTO must ensure that the capital resources, people resources, and system resources of a company are focused on the initiatives and projects that drive revenue, improve cash flow, and increase return on investment. Secondly, a CTO ensures that customers have a positive experience on all levels from when they enter a store, when they pay a bill, or when they upgrade their products. It is important to instill these principles in the front line associates so they understand the relationship between success of the business and their ability to offer a positive experience to customers. As with other executives, a CTO must also repeat and reinforce the company's vision and strategy for all employees in order for the company to be successful. The strength of the overall objectives within the culture of a company is directly linked to the success of the company share value, cash flow, and revenue performance.

Finding Success as a Technology Leader

In order to be successful as a technology leader, an individual must possess skills both in technology and leadership. For the wireless communications industry, an individual must be competent in the core technologies such as IP, data services, and radio frequency technology. He or she must also understand how each of these technologies is evolving with time. Along with the understanding of this technology, a technology leader must possess the ability to simplify these complex, technical developments and trends into strategies a company can implement to increase its market share, improve its bottom line profitability, and increase its revenue. Because the technology in the wireless communication industry is changing rapidly, a technology leader must put the company resources on the technology changes that will build the company's future success. There are some tools a technology leader can use to help identify useful technology and simplify it for business executives.

Because this individual also leads others, he or she must have a high level of honesty, ethics, humility, and integrity in order to set the example every day for the employees he or she leads directly and the ones he or she indirectly influences. Humility is especially important, because technology leaders should recognize that they do not have all the answers and that they are not infallible. As a result, they should seek help in making decisions from their colleagues. With these qualities, a leader can convince others to follow the vision of the company.

Working with Other Executives

As a technology leader, an individual will work closely with the head of marketing and the head of finance in order to align objectives. All three executives must understand the general vision of the company. When dealing with a marketing executive, a technology officer needs to understand the overall product and services objectives of the marketing department and compare them with the overall engineering objectives of the technology department. The two executives should then determine a shared roadmap for the future.

When dealing with the financial officer, a technology officer should understand the overall roadmap of the company in terms of cash flow and align it with the level of investment required by the engineering of new products or the support of them. They must then reconcile any gaps in the overall financial plan of the company and the plan of the technology department.

Team Members

In team members, technology leaders are looking for individuals who are intelligent enough to synthesize information and recognize underlying patterns in the data they are given. Because team members receive information from different data streams, they must be able to recognize the overall patterns that would be useful to drive the business or modify and adjust the business plan. Also, technology leaders search for individuals with a high degree of ethics, honesty, and purpose. Because business is relationship-oriented, they must also have the ability to build relationships with teams within engineering and outside engineering.

Once a technology leader finds individuals with these requirements, he or she must set goals for them. First, technology leaders should clearly present the vision of the company and of the engineering and technology group so team members fully understand both. By getting out in the field on a regular basis, a technology leader can share with them the company's mission and the operating context of that vision. It is also helpful to explain the necessity of certain tasks to meet the company's plan and mission. Then CTOs should collaborate with the different groups to map out the goals and objectives for each group and tie those into the company's overall mission. In general, this is not a static process, so executives should meet quarterly or twice a year to realign the goals of the various groups.

The Biggest Challenges

Rapid change in technology and rapid change in customer expectations is one of the greatest challenges in the wireless communication industry. For example, in many cases a company will deploy a technology that will be virtually obsolete in twelve months. As a result, it is important to sharpen and to adjust forecasts of possible future situations in order to understand what may occur.

Similarly, the most difficult situations involve organizational change such as changing the structure or bringing in new expertise. Human beings in general feel threatened when a new variable is introduced into the mix. The difficulty arises in explaining to people why the change, whether it be organizational or procedural, is necessary. In taking the time to explain, a technology leader can set the example for others to communicate the reasons for the particular change.

In addition, customers now expect a wireless phone to operate like a landline phone anywhere and at any time. In the early days of the industry, cellular companies designed systems to provide coverage in certain locations rather than everywhere. In order to keep pace with the idea that a customers should have service everywhere, companies must invest in places they would not have traditionally. As a result, some of the operating philosophies and principles are changing. As and example, in the early days of cellular, cellular systems where designed to ensure coverage on highways and roads, with little attention given to coverage within buildings, houses, and other indoor venues. The customer's expectations today are that the wireless device work indoors and outdoors. This is requiring cellular service providers to place and locate the cellular towers and base stations in such a way as to ensure superior coverage indoors and outdoors. This change is impacting capital investment strategies, as well as network engineering strategies. Capital that would have been used to improve outdoor coverage is now being diverted to improve indoor coverage. Radio engineers are receiving training on how to address in-building coverage issues, in addition to their regular training.

Another challenge of a CTO is overcoming the misconception that he or she singularly decides which technologies a company should implement. In contrast, the decision of a CTO is based upon the input of a variety of different people and sources. I take credit if the decision is bad; however, I feel compelled to share the credit when a decision is good. The CTO can overcome this misconception by openly recognizing those folks who are a key part in the decision process. The CTO should spend considerable time in the field sharing the company vision and key business strategies. This can provide an excellent opportunity for communication with the key players in the decision-making process, which can help overcome the misconception that the CTO singularly makes decisions concerning technology.

Vital Resources

In order to be successful, CTOs should use a combination of three sources in order to remain abreast of the recent technological developments within an industry. One successful resource is to remain in connection with partners. For example, companies use certain vendors to help them deliver products and services to customers. Critical to maintaining a thriving company is meeting with partners on a regular basis in order to forecast future technology developments and share the direction of their respective organizations in response to the developments. Secondly, a CTO must continuously read technical trade journals, academic journals, and publications around some of the core technologies in order to determine the inflection points of a particular technology. Moreover, the reading should include publications from other disciplines and knowledge domains. This is important, because new ideas and new technologies can be applied in areas for which they were not originally intended. This is extremely powerful. By reading, a CTO can remain abreast of what technology is phasing out and what technology is coming in to replace it. Additionally, a CTO should seek out advice from other CTOs or mentors within the industry. He or she must also be willing to listen and take the advice that is offered.

Expenses

For my team, travel expenses such as spending time meeting front line employees, customers, and partners are an important expense, which I view as in investment. Also, the team spends money assessing the viability of new technologies by conducting various technology trials and pilots. This is very important to determining the potential of a new technology and its ability to enhance, extend, and evolve the company's business strategy.

If a company needs to forecast future trends and better respond the technology trends, it is critically important to obtain technologies in the early stages. This enables the CTO to provide feedback and direction to business providers who provide a critical piece of the new technology, thus influencing the final product deliverable. An example of this strategy in the wireless industry is a service called push to talk for cellular, or PoC. This service allows two or more users of cellular service to communicate with each other like users of walkie-talkies. When the service was originally made available to the wireless carriers, various technical trials identified a number of improvement opportunities that, in the long run, would enhance the customer's experience. These enhancements resulted in a better product and a higher customer retention rate for this service.

Research and Development

First, a company should meet with technology officers from other companies that are not necessarily within its industry to understand what products and services may be developing. It should also meet with its customers to determine their needs and future demands for products and services. By asking these questions, a company can formulate a picture of what the future may look like. Then the company can use technology trials to determine how the developments currently available can become products to meet the needs of customers. Frequently, technologies are paired together in different ways to create a new one. PoC and picture messaging are a good example of this. Cellular phones are now coming standard with the ability to take pictures, because camera technology is integrated with the phone. Cellular phones are also now starting to include PoC service as standard. The wireless industry has come to realize that the PoC technology can be coupled with camera phone capability to create a new service called push-to-X. Push-to-X means users of wireless service can not only use their phones to communicate with each other like walkie-talkies, but they can also push pictures to each other while they are communicating via this mode.

The Changing Role of Technology Leadership

In the past, a technology leader was a hardware guru or software guru who understood technology in the same way as a programmer or hardware designer. Now the technology leader builds relationships, synthesizes information, finds patterns, and communicates objectives, as well as the company's vision and mission. He or she must also simplify the technology so business leaders can make decisions. As a result, technology leaders have become more business savvy and are not as involved in the nitty-gritty details of the underlying technologies as in the past.

In the future, this trend will continue so that technology leaders will become less and less expert in some of the core technologies, rather having more of a big picture understanding of a variety of technologies. They will understand how core technologies fit with other technologies, but will have a more general grasp of these technologies, rather than being an expert in all of them. With the increasing number of new technologies on the horizon, this trend is a practical one for leaders of technology. A technology leader will have to identify the technologies that will drive business, will have to develop a general understanding of those technologies, and will have to learn to jump intelligently from one technology to the next.

In order to prepare for these future trends, CTOs should remember to remain honest with their employees and surround themselves with smart, dedicated, ethical people. In such surroundings, CTOs can be honest with themselves about their own abilities and then divvy responsibilities accordingly. Also, they should not take themselves too seriously, but remember to have fun through it all.

Michael S. Irizarry joined U.S. Cellular in February of 2002 as executive vice president of engineering and chief technology officer. Mr. Irizarry comes to U.S. Cellular from Verizon Wireless, where he served as vice president of network and was responsible for managing the company's Midwest area wireless network, which spanned fifteen states, serving 8.5 million subscribers. He also served as executive director of network operations for the Southeast region of Bell Atlantic Mobile, and has held positions in engineering and engineering management for companies such as Paging Network Inc. and Motorola.

Mr. Irizarry is a senior member of the Institute of Electrical and Electronics Engineers (IEEE), the IEEE Communications Society, and the IEEE Computer Society. Additionally, he is an FCC-licensed general class radio operator, and an FCC-licensed extra class amateur radio operator—AB4KJ. Mr. Irizarry resides in Algonquin, Illinois with his wife, Christine, their four children, Renee, Leni, Ian, and Shannon, and their two dogs, Biscuit and Mina.

Overcoming Challenges and Building a Strong Team

Russ Rosen

Chief Information Officer

Rooms to Go

Goals and Responsibilities

The first goal of a chief information officer (CIO) is to ensure that all the existing systems and processes are functioning properly. In doing so, he or she ensures that the company will not be negatively impacted as a result of system failure. The next goal is to implement new technologies to make the company more profitable. These technologies include new software applications, new hardware, any technology that makes existing processes more efficient, and any technology used to decrease the time spent on legacy applications.

A CIO is also responsible for maintaining the information technology (IT) talent level and training of staff. He or she must ensure that the staff is trained in using all new technology and is actively aware of recent technological advances. Lastly, he or she negotiates the price on any new technologies.

Working with Others

I work closest with the chief operating officer, because the greatest opportunity for advancement and efficiency gains is in the operations area. For example, new technology could improve the retail distribution, warehouse operations, or delivery methods of a company. For all executives, a CIO should encourage them to use the technology available to them and propose new ways technology can improve profitability.

The goal of all executives is to increase the profitability of the company. The CIO needs to work with the other business units to find ways to increase sales or reduce costs.

Team Members

Depending on the team, I look for a variety of skills. For a help desk employee, for example, an individual must possess interpersonal skills that enable them to interact with other users. In contrast, I look for technology expertise, flexibility, and self-motivation when trying to fill a more technical position.

The goals of the team are also determined by the area of IT in which a team works, and by the specific duties of the individuals involved. Some team members can be measured by deadlines, while others can be measured by the quantity of tasks completed or by the number of help desk calls taken and resolved. The best advice for team members is to treat the non-IT members of the organization as customers. The IT department exists to service the other areas of the organization.

At Rooms to Go, no formal checks and balances system exists, but instead the company evaluates its employees in an annual review. Ultimately, the team is evaluated by the profitability of the entire company, because all bonuses at the end of the year are a factor of that profitability. As a result, a technology leader should update employees on a monthly basis as to how the company is performing. Then the team leaders can set the goals for their individual groups.

Strategies for Success

A successful technology leader works to align the IT goals with the goals of the chief executive officer and chief financial officer. In general, individuals believe an IT leader is an individual with no business knowledge or interpersonal skills; however, the current function of the position is more management-based and deals more with understanding the business than the technology side. A CIO must create goals that are relevant to the bottom line of the company and that make the company more profitable. It is important to have the support of the executive board on all IT projects. In order to encourage this working relationship, a CIO must demonstrate that he or she can create value for the company through the use of technology. As a result, a CIO can gain the visibility with the other C-level executives in the company.

Another component necessary for a successful CIO is having the right employees. He or she must recognize talent and obtain the right mix of people to maintain the IT organization. It is also important for CIOs to empower and encourage their employees to do their jobs more effectively and efficiently. Employees should remain focused in order to meet any unexpected challenges. A CIO should always acknowledge excellent work and provide incentives that motivate employees. Possible incentives include days off, dinners, or baseball game tickets.

The better technology leaders are the ones who understand how technology can help business instead of those who understand technology only for the sake of technology. For example, I implemented a business intelligence tool used by buyer personnel that evaluates who a customer is and what they buy. From a business perspective, this technology allows executives to make more informed decisions about advertising or the furniture to stock in a store.

A strategy that was successful for Rooms to Go was aligning technology with store operations. In order to do so, a position within the IT department called a "store liaison" was created. This individual's function is to interact with the stores on a daily basis in order to identify the pros and cons of available technologies. The store liaison identifies the needs of the store and makes personnel jobs more efficient. This individual also assists in implementing and training individuals for new technology.

Challenges of a CIO

The general resistance to change is the most challenging aspect of being a CIO. Because employees become accustomed to doing their jobs one way, they are often reluctant to change their methods. In order to implement a new technology or process, a CIO must be good at training and reinforcing the benefit of the new technology. You need to help the employees envision what their duties will be like once they get past the initial disruption so they can see the future benefits.

Another challenge is the failure of a system at the warehouse or store level. These failures hinder the livelihood of the employees at stores because they cannot make money if the systems are down and hinder them from making a sale. Also, any situation that occurs as a result of a system failure poses a challenge. In this situation, all IT personnel are on call at any hour, because emphasis is placed on evaluating and solving the problem quickly.

Expenses

The cost of maintenance is frequently high and is hard to reduce because these costs provide assurance that all systems will continue to run properly. Retail companies also spend money to ensure that they have response times at all hours and spend money on backup communication lines to all stores and facilities. System failure at the store level will result in an unsatisfactory customer experience. The perception that a store is unpleasant to shop in is a death sentence for a retailer. The biggest expense, however, is to ensure the reliability of the system. As the value of IT is more positively perceived, the IT budgets will continue to increase. The purchase and successful implementation of system and network performance tools can aid in curtailing expenses over time.

Resources

Because research and development is not a formal department in our organization, we rely on the resource of the employees to suggest new ideas. Once a useful idea is suggested, the affected departments are interviewed to gain their insight as to whether or not the idea is feasible. Then a pilot study is conducted in a controlled environment to evaluate the benefits of that technology.

Another resource used by a high-profile retailer is the publicity around the name. Technology leaders use this resource to their advantage by negotiating discounts they can get by trading off with a high-profile name.

It is important to keep up with the trade magazines to monitor the new technologies that may be emerging, as well as to see what the competition is using in their environment.

The Changing Face of Technology Leadership

The technology leader of a company is more of a business leader than a technology specialist. The more successful CIOs will be the individuals who know business first and then know how to implement the technology to fit the business. It is more difficult to come from the technology side and then try to understand the business. As a result, technology leadership positions will go more to business leaders who do not necessarily have a technology background. Because any leadership within an organization can change, an individual must know how that change will affect his or her role as a technology leader, and must adapt to that change if necessary.

In order to handle these changes in the future, remember three golden rules of being a technology leader. First, CIOs should make themselves visible in the organization by interacting with executives in the board room. Secondly, they surround themselves with the right mix of talent in an environment that fosters learning and improvement. And finally, CIOs should be pioneers rather than dinosaurs. They must remain aware of the latest technological developments in order to gain or maintain an advantage over a company's competitors.

It is important that any new technologies that are implemented are scalable. In this day of mergers and acquisitions, your environmental variables can change rapidly. One of the last things the executive board considers during the merger/acquisition decision process is the effect on IT, but in reality it should be close to the top of the list. You must be agile.

Russ Rosen has been with Rooms to Go as the lead information technology individual since 1991 when the company was founded. Rooms to Go is the nation's largest furniture retailer in terms of sales, exceeding $1.3 billion annually. The company has over a hundred showrooms in seven states, plus an online presence that services most of the United States.

Mr. Rosen graduated with a B.S. in computer science from Renssalear Polytechnic Institute in Troy, New York in 1986. He began his career as a project manager/programmer for Verticomp Inc. in Chelmsford, Massachusetts and then moved on to Rooms to Go five years later.

A Look at Technology in the Childcare Industry

Timothy Young
Vice President, Information Technology
Bright Horizons Family Solutions

My Technology Vision

As the vice president of information technology (IT), I am charged with the company's technology vision strategy in developing the business relationships with the communities we serve (i.e., our employees) on a global level. At the foundation of this is building a cohesive and unified team, which serves as a resource to these communities, assisting them with the realization and creation of new and innovative solutions to meet their needs.

For example, in our industry—childcare and education—our job begins and ends with taking care of children and working with the parents we serve. At the end of the day, we strive to meet their needs from a customer service level and from a technology standpoint. We have a unique ideology in leveraging customer service. As a technology leader in the childcare and education industry, it is vital to adopt the same high levels of customer service within the team as expected by the many parents we serve. As we strive to nurture each child's unique qualities and potential, it's critical to be connected with the constituents we serve. We have to be held at the same level of accountability in customer service that our employees are at the center level.

We operate in a multi-country and highly distributed environment. Our world headquarters consists of more than 200 employees, but we have an overall employee base of over 16,000 worldwide. Leveraging technology that enhances communication is critical in our business. We need to streamline and ease access to information, data collection, and how we aggregate that data. We strive to leverage a very simplified and unified user experience through all of our applications. We are currently moving all systems toward a Web experience, so we base everything around a Web application.

Selfless Leadership

Having the necessary hands-on field experience and breadth of knowledge about how technology is woven into the overall strategic plan of any business is essential, but I feel that leadership has to be defined separately from management. Any leader has to balance and manage relationships.

Leadership and management are not synonymous: leading is about change, influencing others to change, and building relationships with communities such as your own team, fellow executives, and constituents.

The only effective way to achieve this is to become selfless, placing more value on others than yourself. An interesting dynamic occurs when you discover, believe, and live this style of leadership: it will create a team that will walk through fire with you. You become a builder of relationships. There are two quotations central to this way of leading. First, "Do nothing from selfishness or empty conceit; but with humility of mind, let each of you regard one another as more important than himself. Do not merely look out for your own personal interests, but also for the interests of others." Second, "The beginning of leadership is a battle for the hearts and minds of others." The end product of this attitude is trustworthiness and credibility.

A successful leader must also understand the importance of nurturing a team environment and getting that team to rally around a common set of goals and purpose. One example is an internal guide we have developed to help us with this, called our "IT Creed," which comprises:

1. Understand the landscape. It is essential for us to be knowledgeable about our industry and environment, and to be able to leverage the key decision makers.
2. Embrace the vision for how IT will help build the company's success. It is very important for us to embrace this vision for aligning the business goals and technology.
3. Shape and create opportunity. We need to make every effort to identify the business needs, strategy, and its drivers to be able to communicate the IT strategy required to address those needs.
4. Demonstrate clear IT governance. This will enable us to better align business and IT strategies, which will help us to consistently build credibility and trust.
5. Sustain a dynamic IT organization, one that is more efficient and focused. Maintain excellence in customer service and sustain both strategic and financial foundations.
6. Encourage and develop a high-performing team. We need to understand the competencies required for this dynamic team, one

at relies much more on building solid relationships and strives to gain knowledge for greater effectiveness within the company.

7. Manage the global enterprise in IT risks. We have to be aware of the risks and need to facilitate the management of them across the global enterprise, and we must all lead and take responsibility for this process.

8. Communicate IT performance in a business-relevant language and be able to communicate how IT is contributing to the success and growth of the business using non-technical terminology.

I hold my entire management team accountable to these points. I think it's critical that the IT team be a true partner within the organization as a professional service provider, and build relationships with communities, our fellow executives, and the constituents we serve.

This year, we developed an IT vision concept that supports this, called the "TEAM Philosophy":

- "T" is technology. We align with the business goals of the company, have a consistent unified project strategy, and strengthen the infrastructure.

- "E" is efficiency. Personal development within our team. The growth of the department and growth of the company don't typically occur at a parallel rate, which is why identifying efficiencies within a team are essential.

- "A" is attitude. This intersects with personal development, company principles, and the departmental mission statement. We take the company mission statement and see where it is relevant for the IT team. We are solution-oriented, we have to have a "no excuse" mentality, and we ensure that customer service is key.

- "M" is measure results. We look at performance in everything we do, and we always take a step back and see the lessons learned. We try to enhance systems and reporting, and we are consistent with annual reviews.

The Most Significant Challenges

One of the most challenging aspects of being a technology leader is the landscape, which is always changing both internally and externally. A successful technology leader must have the ability to anticipate, adapt, and build a global IT vision. One must also build a team and an infrastructure that support the ever-increasing demands of the enterprises and realize fast-paced, dynamic growth. We are seeing incredible growth within our company, and looking at a plan for doubling in the next five years. This is extremely difficult without a strong, cohesive team that operates with a single, consistent vision for supporting IT infrastructure. An IT leader is only as strong as his or her team. You have to build upon the solid rock of an excellent team and solid infrastructure; leaders who don't realize this are building teams on sinking sand, and won't be able to weather the storms when they come.

I see a paradigm shift going on within IT: IT no longer owns 100 percent of the technology piece, and we have to learn to adopt a partnership model. It has always been efficient to understand a person's position, but when the overall IT team has a clear understanding of the vision and how to effectively align technology within the vision, everything seems to cascade into place. The natural progression is that soon, IT won't have to exert energy to position itself with the executives; instead, the executives will instinctively invite IT to the table, because they are viewed as an equal partner in the success of the company.

My IT Team

I see potential leadership qualities in all positions in a team, so I look for the aforementioned leadership qualities in every member of my team. I always communicate that technology is inherent in IT, it's a given—but customer service is something you cannot teach someone: it's either in their fabric, or it isn't.

We accomplish this in a few ways. There is an overall growth and learning process within the company, which helps facilitate goals on a high level. We also bundle assessment tools to create an individual learning path for every employee. Specifically within IT, all the IT managers are held accountable to the IT Creed, and we continue to self-assess ourselves with 360-degree reviews, field surveys, and so on.

I continually tell my team members to not let their jobs consume them. I am a strong advocate of work/life balance. I say everybody's family comes before their job. I view my team members as people like myself: we all have needs, we all require feedback, and we all need to be treated with respect. I take interest in and get to know each member of my team on an individual level.

The advice that has had the most significant impact on me has been learned through experience. The many truths and guidance I have found from inspirational sources are:

- Leaders influence others.
- Everything rises and falls on the leader.
- Leaders take full responsibility for everything.
- The essential ingredient for leadership is credibility.
- Leaders must possess tremendous trust in people.
- Leaders need to be teachable.
- Great leaders are effective communicators of vision.
- Great leadership is always assisted by other people.

As the IT team has evolved into a strategic and valued player in the overall business strategy, we present ourselves as a genesis of almost all initiatives within the company. Just about every facet of what we do somehow intersects with technology, and over the years we have redefined our team into what I refer to as three verticals. We are decoupling ourselves from the organizational chart, and we sliced IT up into three vertical silos, which correspond to the reporting roles within the organizational chart:

1. Infrastructure
2. Telecommunications
3. Business technology

We have defined horizontal roles that are sliced through these silos. We have also adapted a "heads-up display" model. We do this within the team and outside the team, and this allows us to single out the five to statistics we need to look at to successfully complete our tasks.

Team Spending and Research and Development

There are two significant areas of IT expenses. The first is in general and administrative, with salaries and benefits, and the other is capital. We have become fairly proficient of being within budget every year, but we have put more into people and resources. We recognize and reward people who are really embracing the IT Creed; once we have a good IT team, we typically decide whether to increase salaries, add bonuses, or offer stock options. We invest in our people.

We leverage a lot of resources to help us with research and development, but we always leverage with a team approach. In most cases, I am describing a team with boundaries that extend beyond the IT team: an IT team that thinks it owns the entire technology slice won't survive long.

Some of the most useful resources I find are online. I also tap into established networks of people and vendors, and embrace the partnership model. I specifically mention those vendors who embrace the partnership model, because they become integrated and trusted advisors. Vendors who understand our business needs can consistently provide us with personalized enterprise solutions, which help us achieve our business goals on a global level. They are a tremendous resource.

The Maverick Syndrome

One major challenge is a trend toward clusters of self-centered behavior. This manifests itself in the form of silos, which are only concerned with their own issues: it's the Maverick Syndrome. This makes it challenging to get these clusters on the same page, and to effectively leverage resources on an acceptable level. This can hinder departmental teams from getting in line with the growth rate of the company.

Technology Leadership

Establishing good, partner-orientated relationships with executives and the constituency are all connected to good IT leadership. True IT leadership means learning how to become and stay selfless. This selflessness will ripen the fruits of your team, and the harvest will be vast. Everything falls into place when you embrace and live this concept: find a way to become a selfless leader, always putting others first. This means you become the lightening rod for the team. When things go wrong, have their backs; never take credit for the contributions and efforts realized within the team; and always promote them in every circle you travel in. This creates trustworthiness and credibility, and will bear rich fruit.

Timothy Young is charged with Bright Horizons Family Solutions' technology vision strategy in developing business relationships with the communities served on a global level.

Prior to joining Bright Horizons, Mr. Young was employed at NSC Corporation (a division of Waste Management), as the manager of information technology for all of NCS's United States operations.

Mr. Young holds a B.S. degree from Fitchburg State Collage. Other affiliations include HP Interex, National Collegiate Computer Science Award, National Collegiate Business Merit Award, All American Scholars Award, and Who's Who in American Colleges and Universities.

Dedication:
My Lord and Savior
Danae and Joshua
My family
Curtis Flory Sr.
Ray Hendrickson
My assistant, Alexa Warburton

Technology Management in Higher Education

David J. Gray

Vice President of Information Technology, Chief Information Officer, and Chief Executive Officer, UMassOnline

University of Massachusetts

Technology Management Goals

The main goal of a technology management leader is to provide a high quality of service to the customers of the information technology (IT) service organization. The specialist has to provide cost-effective, high-quality services to those customers and provide a model for integration of services. The successful technology management leader must have the ability to persuade, to be a diplomat, to market ideas, and to understand and support the business requirements of his or her organization. He or she must possess the ability to communicate effectively and to sell people on their vision. Their achievement is predicated on their ability to market their ideas effectively.

A Role of a Technology Leader in Higher Education

The art of being a technology leader in higher education is different than working in the commercial world. Higher education is all about collaboration and building consensus. Colleges and universities tend to be consensus-driven institutions where progress is based on one's ability to motivate people to see a shared vision, to engage them in the development of strategy, and to make sure their perspective on service is taken into account. Unlike other organizations, higher education is not very hierarchical. In other words, "command and control" does not work nearly as effectively as "convince and cooperate." In order for technology management to be effective, the IT team must be engaged with their customers, understand the customers' needs, and help make sure those needs are fulfilled.

Traditional higher education institutions are nonprofit by definition and thus are not motivated by profit. Their motivation and mission is service-oriented. Technology management must pay attention to the core mission of their institutions and align with that mission. As do their institutions, they need to be incredibly service-oriented. This is the first prerequisite for IT leaders in higher education. Success is determined not by returning a profit, but by whether or not the team is providing quality service to the university's faculty, students, and staff.

The Road to Success

Technology management strategies are mostly built around trying to build a shared sense of direction, of working toward a common vision and portfolio of services. The strategic dimension is to get people to see that the way the team wants to proceed is in the university's best interest. In a multi-campus university like the University of Massachusetts, this determination of interest is even more complex. For example, there is always an option for campuses to choose to offer services locally as opposed to offering them across the entire university system. The technology management team would have to demonstrate a compelling business argument for the campuses to yield their autonomy. The team could offer the benefit of being able to offer services at a reduced cost and/or being able to provide higher-quality services. A leveraging argument can also be advanced that better services can be obtained by taking advantage of certain economies of scale to bring more resources to bear on the production of those services. In many instances, the concentration and focusing of resources yields greater organizational effectiveness than the diffusion of resources across multiple locations.

The most demanding aspect of bringing individual campuses together to contend with enterprise-wide matters is dealing with the distinct leaders of each local campus. Frequently, they come to the table with divergent viewpoints, priorities, management styles, and concerns. Trying to move them toward consensus and getting them on the same page is an incredible challenge, because their default position is almost always going to be to perform and manage services locally. An effective leader in this scenario must demonstrate convincingly to them why it would make sense to give up producing services locally in order to produce them centrally. It is seldom easy to persuade people from different places with different challenges and needs to see the common need and good that can be developed through collaboration on IT projects, services, or initiatives.

Financial Impact

The management of IT in higher education has a direct financial impact on the university system. In many cases, the human resources, student, and financial applications are operated centrally. The provision of those services is what enables the university to transact business, to effectively serve their students, and to support the instructional activities of the faculty. This very crucial set of support services is related to the core mission of instruction, research, and public service. Contemporary Web-based applications that offer self-service to the varied members of a university community are expensive both to implement and maintain. The IT skill sets required to manage complex projects and to maintain complex, integrated systems are increasingly in demand and, hence, more costly than even a few years ago. While it may be tempting for some institutions to consider controlling costs by hanging on to legacy systems a few years longer or by not providing a technology-rich environment for their campus communities, such a course would likely be a classic example of "penny-wise, pound-foolish." Institutions that fail to offer their constituents high-quality, technology-based services will be at a competitive disadvantage and stand to lose far more in revenue from lost customers than they might gain through controlling costs. An increasing part of effective IT leadership is advocating for the proper level of resources to assure that the institution is well-positioned competitively.

The IT Team

The skills of collaboration and salesmanship are frequently in use among the rest of the central IT team. This allows the team to work with campus counterparts effectively in a shared services model. In addition to having serious and well-developed technical skills and abilities, the team must have the ability to forge consensus where it may not exist, and to work in a collaborative fashion. They have to be able to do this not only with their staff associates from the central IT department, but with the clients they work with as well.

The best way to achieve goals is to set them as a team. Goals that are shared will prevail over those that are imposed. One example of a way to do this is to hold strategic retreats where the sole purpose is to develop strategic goals. The team would then need to come to consensus on more precise objectives that will lead to goal attainment and to establish priorities. The stated objectives must be framed in ways that are measurable. In that way, people and project teams can be held accountable for producing results that move the company or university toward attainment of those objectives and the strategic goals they support.

Team members who work in higher education need to have patience. The university environment is not one that typically yields rapid results or instant gratification. IT does not operate as a hierarchical command structure in most universities because of the many power centers the university is likely to have. The very need to build consensus across many campuses (and departments within campuses) frequently slows down decision-making processes. As a consequence, progress comes in smaller increments and it takes longer to produce results. It is very important for members of a team to understand their environment and not get frustrated by it. They must develop a high degree of patience in terms of making progress and moving things ahead. Noteworthy results and progress are made, but there is an overhead price to be paid for the collaborative model universities use. It often takes much longer to bring a project to completion because a team might have to gain agreement from many different campuses or units in order to even begin a project.

Keeping the Team Informed

It is important that the team sit down together to give progress updates on strategic goals and objectives. It is necessary for the entire management group to understand the progress that is being made, to know if any members of the group are experiencing any difficulties or challenges, and to engage each other in dialogue about new strategic initiatives. Every member of the team should feel some ownership of the process and the results. All forms of communication—oral, hard copy, Web-based, and e-mail—must be exploited.

The Human Expense

The single biggest expense in terms of technology management is personnel. Substantial human resource expenses are necessary to build a high-performance professional team. Technology professionals in an increasingly information-centric society are highly compensated individuals, and there must be concern about recruitment and retention of those employees. Human resource costs are going to be the dominant part of any large-scale IT organization for quite some time. There will always be other expenses—for example, capital items such as the lifecycle renewal of server infrastructure, storage, and networking equipment—but personnel will always be the largest expenditure and *the most important asset* of the IT organization. Because this asset is portable and possesses free will, it must be accorded the highest priority.

Research and Development

The best practice for research and development is to ask all members of a team, in particular senior managers, to keep an eye on the horizon and to do environmental scanning. That entails both looking at new technologies as they come across the radar screen for potential application within the business, and looking at and benchmarking against competition to understand what they are doing. If at all possible, build a component for research and development into your IT organization's budget and be prepared to fund small pilot or demonstration projects involving the use of new technologies.

Supply and Demand

The most difficult situation in terms of technology management would be the matching of resource constraints against service demands. There is frequently a mismatch of demand for resources and an appetite for services that may outstrip a company's ability to supply it. A company may not have the finances to do all it would like to do. The company might have to make some difficult financial choices regarding projects it would like to take on but does not have the organizational bandwidth to accommodate. They might want to scale up existing services in an even more robust way and offer better customer service but, again, financial constraints might preclude them from doing so. In an ideal world, financially driven cost constraints would not exist. In the real world we all inhabit, however, the establishment of priorities to balance the supply and demand equation is essential.

Majority Rule

An enormous hurdle to overcome in terms of business is that, in many instances, the client wants to achieve closure on issues faster than the company is able to, and there are times when not everybody is on the same page. Unless there is a critical mass of people firmly behind major IT strategic initiatives or projects, it becomes very difficult to move forward. Many people get frustrated by the lack of progress toward goals they see as self-evident, and they aren't mindful of the fact that not having like-minded critical players in agreement could well mean that the goal is ultimately unattainable. More so in higher education, governmental, and nonprofit organizations than perhaps commercial environments, majority rule is a fact of life. Leaders, however, must remind themselves that majorities may be forged; a test of leadership is building the critical mass of opinion to permit organizational progress.

Staying Ahead

It has become a great challenge to stay abreast of change in technology. So much is happening across so many different technological fronts that it is tough to keep all developments straight; as important is discerning where new technologies might intersect and pose synergistic opportunities for organizations. Keeping an eye toward goals that have already been established is increasingly complex. One challenge for technology leaders with finite resources is that they can't be all things to all people. They have to make some tough judgment calls and live with the consequences.

Technology leadership is going to become even more closely aligned with the delivery of value to the core business. In higher education, one of the challenges is delivering even more value to the academic core. In recent years, universities have spent substantial resources on building administrative support infrastructures, and those activities have consumed the predominant share of attention and capital. While the administrative infrastructure is very important, the focus of resources there has come at the expense of focusing on our core business. A big challenge and change on the horizon for institutions of higher learning is going to be the shift and focus from administrative and support technologies to technologies that will help drive improvements in how they deliver the core business of scholarship—i.e., teaching, learning, and research.

Golden Rules

There are three golden rules to being a leader in technology. The first rule is to provide the highest-quality customer service. The better the service, the more repeat business a company will earn. The second rule is to build high-performance teams that are accountable for the products and services they support. The third rule is to strive for continuous improvement. This imperative pertains at both the individual and corporate levels.

David J. Gray has served as vice president for information technology and chief information officer for the University of Massachusetts since September of 2000. In this capacity, Mr. Gray coordinates and facilitates information technology planning, integration, and training across all university functions. He provides leadership in the planning, acquisition, and implementation of information and instructional/administrative technologies.

Mr. Gray provides day-to-day oversight of University Information Technology Services (UITS), the University's administrative information technology organization. UITS is responsible for the provision of high-quality computing and information systems support to the five UMass campuses and the president's office. In addition, UITS provides leadership and management support for the Massachusetts Information Turnpike Initiative (MITI), through which advanced network services are provided to the Massachusetts public higher education community and other constituents. Mr. Gray also provides oversight to the university's PeopleSoft enterprise resource planning initiative, through which the five campuses and the president's office created a shared information systems environment that addresses the financial, human resource, and student information systems needs of the university in a highly integrated manner.

In September of 2003, President Jack Wilson, founding chief executive officer of UMassOnline, asked Mr. Gray additionally to serve as interim chief executive officer of UMassOnline, the university's five-campus distance learning initiative. In May of 2004, President Wilson appointed Mr. Gray to the chief executive officer post on a permanent basis. He continues to serve as vice president and chief information officer. During his tenure as chief executive officer for UMassOnline, Mr. Gray has overseen the successful transition to a new generation of e-learning infrastructure, centered around WebCT's Vista enterprise learning management system. UMassOnline, under his leadership, has also concluded a successful system-wide strategic planning initiative that will assure the maturation and continued growth and success of New England's premier online learning venture.

Prior to joining the University of Massachusetts, Mr. Gray served as the vice chancellor for information technology for the Pennsylvania State System of Higher Education for five years. In this capacity, Mr. Gray provided leadership to the formation of the Keystone Library Network, a virtual library service linking the fourteen state system campuses and the State Library of Pennsylvania. Mr. Gray also led the establishment of the system's Center for Distance Education and served as principal architect of the system's instructional technology plan, adopted by the board of governors in April of 1999. In addition, Mr. Gray represented the state system on the board of directors of the Pennsylvania Technology Investment Authority, a group empowered to strategically invest state funds in economic development and university research initiatives. Previously, Mr. Gray served the Pennsylvania States System as assistant vice chancellor for financial management and in other administrative leadership posts since 1983.

Mr. Gray earned a bachelor's degree in political science and a master of public administration degree from the Pennsylvania State University in University Park, Pennsylvania. He has been active in EDUCAUSE and NACUBO, and a variety of professional and community service organizations. Mr. Gray resides in Westborough, Massachusetts with his wife, Margaret, and two children.

The Technology Leader: Part Technologist, Part Businessman, Part Psychologist

Christopher R. Barber

Senior Vice President and Chief Information Officer

WesCorp

Goals of a Technology Leader

The first goal of a technology leader is to create a collaborative environment for the information technology (IT) team by developing a team mentality that increases productivity and IT staff satisfaction. It is also important for a technology leader to manage the expectations of his or her team and throughout the organization. From a political and professional standpoint, it is damaging to become overzealous or over-promise on a project that does not deliver the expected results. The second goal involves using this productive, team-oriented IT staff to discover innovative solutions that give a company competitive advantage over its competition. These solutions then increase efficiencies throughout the enterprise. For example, the creation of low-cost customer self-service e-channel solutions. The third goal of a technology leader is to provide intelligent views of high-valued data that allows executives to make intelligent business decisions.

Qualities of a Successful Technology Leader

A technology leader should be part technologist, part businessman, and part psychologist. First, you need to understand technology to lead a technology group. Second, you need to understand the business to know how to properly apply the technology. And third, you need to be a psychologist to understand and influence your peers in the organization.

The role of a chief information officer (CIO) or an IT leader has changed. The CIO role has changed as a result of businesses understanding that technology can help cut costs, increase efficiency, and provide a better product than the competition. Because of this, the CEO looks to the technology leaders to help identify these technologies, and therefore, like it or not, the CIO now has to have a seat at the executive table. A job of a technology leader is to make certain the management staff understands that the technology organization can provide a company with the infrastructure, the tools, and the ideas (strategy) to allow them to best perform their jobs. As a result, he or she must understand business and the business needs of a company in order to align those needs with the available technology.

Interacting with Other Executives

A technology leader typically works with senior-level staff such as the chief investment officer, chief executive officer, chief financial officer, and senior vice presidents of areas like business development and payment systems. In this relationship, a technology leader must understand the viewpoint of the individual players and know how to influence him or her. Analyzing these individuals to identify their pressure points helps a technology leader pursue actions that benefit the company. This analysis is also important because an individual's point of view often favors a certain presentation style. Some individuals can understand information through verbal communication, while others require complete presentation with charts and graphs.

Another method to managing this relationship is attempting to encourage business units to initiate an idea rather than IT initiating it. A technology leader should ask questions of business units that eventually lead them to recognizing how a specific technology can help the business. In my organization, IT submitted an idea for what we called a relationship manager workbench. Using portal technology, we thought it would be useful to give the relationship manager a composite view of high-value data from our customer relationship management system so they were able to make fast, intelligent decisions without having to go to multiple places and applications. The idea was extremely well received, but I needed a business unit to push to get it done. It would not be as valuable if I were to push the idea, but if the business unit leader says he or she needs this tool to improve sales, that will get it the resources it needs.

Team Members

An integral quality required of team members in the credit union industry is adaptability. A company can teach new team members skills, but an adaptable personality is a skill that cannot be taught. Very often, project priorities can change, and the team must be able to change directions just as quickly. It is important for team members to focus less on operations and more on larger, overall strategies. They must recognize that permanent change is slow change. Even though change will not occur instantaneously in our industry, progress is still being made if it is viewed over a longer period of time.

For these team members, the goals of a team are dictated by the strategic initiatives for the year. These goals are frequently relative, because the credit union industry involves moving targets. In order to provide some structure, however, the overall goals are managed by the project management organization. Monthly meetings are conducted to review how the business relationship is managed, to identify new projects, to acknowledge milestones that were hit, and to discuss why objectives are not being met if necessary.

A way to monitor the status of projects is completing a project status report that is submitted to the project management organization. These reports identify the progress made on a particular project, as well as report any issues that have arisen. They also include the original timeline of the project and the comparative progress on that timeline. If a project is behind, the report also attempts to explain why. For example, the requirement for a project may have changed, or issues involving IT or resources could have arisen.

Key Strategies

From a strategic standpoint, a business leader should manage projects to engage the whole organization in understanding that technology adds value to the business and supports the objectives of the company. By prioritizing and managing projects in this way, a technology leader can garner the support of the business units on any project. One example of a project that is useful to business units is consolidating information and business intelligence tools into an informational data storage that provides businesspeople with the right information at the right time to the right desktop. This information helps business executives make informed decisions about high-value assets.

Another successful strategy involves creating a business relationship management team to develop a business relationship with each of the business units. In this relationship, a management team should strive to understand the business needs of a company, should meet with business units on a weekly basis to go over projects or issues, and should update them on current projects and issues. It is important to market the value of IT and its products.

Overcoming Challenges

In the current environment, it is important to produce more solutions than in the past, despite having fewer resources. It is challenging to maintain a happy, productive staff with this amount of resources. You overcome these obstacles by empowering your staff, pushing decisions down to their lowest level possible thus removing unnecessary bureaucracy, being flexible on staff schedules, celebrating successes, and making sure the IT leaders are available and visible.

Another challenge is understanding the needs of an organization and understanding its business clients, and then aligning them with technology. However, the business units do not have to understand technology or the business of IT. A technology leader must also understand each and every business in the organization, while most business units only need to understand their own line of business. As a result, learning about the business is solely the responsibility of a technology leader and his or her team. The best way I learn a business is by developing a relationship with each business leader and regularly attending their meetings, thereby keeping up to date on their activities.

Handling difficult situations that are people-related also proves to be a challenge for a technology leader. Using the psychologist function of being a technology leader, a leader should be empathetic to both individuals, should resolve the issue in a way that is beneficial to both parties, and should involve each individual in creating that resolution. In order to overcome this challenge, a technology leader must understand the perspectives and motivations of each individual so he or she can navigate around and through conflicts.

Because the role of a technology leader is frequently misunderstood, he or she has the challenge of overcoming misconceptions about his or her function in the organization. The biggest misconception is that a technology leader can provide instant solutions to all business problems. In reality, however, a technology leader possesses general information about a wide variety of subjects, but has expertise in relatively few areas. For example, the chief investment officer understands investments better than the technology leader. As a result, a technology leader may not alone be the best person to determine which software systems are the best for any particular investment need, but must collaborate with the chief investment office. In overcoming this misconception, I believe executives should understand the difference between revolutionary and evolutionary. For instance, the company that implements an automated bulletin board trading system is not revolutionary, but evolutionary because electronic trading was just the next logical step.

The credit union industry also offers its own unique challenges. In contrast to many other industries, the industry is unique because it is composed of organizations that do not operate for profit. Sometimes, executives take actions that are not profitable because those actions best serve the needs of the customers/members. This strategy is often challenging to employees who worked in other industries previously. In general, the credit union industry also has little turnover in its IT staff and in its business staff. As a result, it is challenging to keep a staff trained in current technology without the constant fluctuation between people leaving and people arriving with new skill sets.

Expenses

The largest expense for the company is salaries and benefits. Leadership training and reimbursement for education are also two areas that involve large expenses. The IT leadership team works with its staff to become one team rather than particular teams such as the network team or the software development team. All employees in the IT organization should feel the success of a particular project, regardless of whether it is a data project or a software project. The entire department is encouraged to act as a whole, since it is seen as a whole by the business units. We all sign up for each others' success and march to the mantra of "the power of one."

In addition, we spend money on conferences, travel, data and voice lines, infrastructure, and security.

Research and Development

For research and development, many companies do not have a formal department or process. Instead, they travel, attend conferences, and network with other technology leaders. Another resource is magazines targeted at technology leaders or at specific technologies. Through these resources, a CTO or a chief information officer (CIO) can follow the industry.

Another important resource for research and development is a talented staff. Subject area experts can offer valuable information about specific technologies. It is also important to have contacts throughout an organization to help promote ideas or information. These individuals can encourage business units to pursue a certain project or solution.

It is also valuable to approach research by first identifying a problem and then finding a solution, rather than finding a solution and searching for a place to apply it. For example, the company recently developed and implemented a check imaging solution for retail credit unions. This system allows a retail credit union to scan checks at their branch and transmit the image instead of having to send the physical check for processing. If necessary, the check can be reprinted from the image, providing for a new negotiable legal instrument called a "substitute check." This was all in support of the new legislation referred to as Check 21. Because the industry was becoming more digital, the company predicted that more checks would become digital in some form as well. As a result, it implemented this check repository system to address that need.

Technology Leadership's Changing Role

Technology leadership will continue to be a more collaborative process between technology and the businesses as customers. Technology leaders need to be able to realign the skills of being a technologist to being a business technologist. CIOs are no longer solely focused on technology. Instead, a CTO is focused on technology while the CIO focuses on being more of a business strategist. As a result, CIOs and IT leaders need to be able to market themselves to the rest of the organization by communicating the value of IT to the company and to specific departments within the company. In order to be successful as the role of a CIO continues to change, an individual must remember three golden rules: be patient with others, be empathetic to the needs of the business units, and be an articulate leader that sets an example for others.

Christopher R. Barber is senior vice president and chief information officer at WesCorp, a corporate credit union headquartered in San Dimas, California. WesCorp is a financial services company with more than $25 billion in assets.

At WesCorp, Mr. Barber is responsible for the leadership, strategic direction, and creation of a visionary approach designed to align information technology and business development in support of the company's strategic initiatives. Mr. Barber has more than eighteen years of experience leading strategic development and implementation in the financial services and investment technology arenas.

Prior to joining WesCorp, Mr. Barber served as senior vice president and chief information officer for GlobeNet Capital Corporation in Orlando, Florida. He also held leadership positions with Vector Securities as senior technology officer and with Mercer Investment Consulting as the director of software development for their global resource group.

Mr. Barber received his M.B.A. in finance from DePaul University and his bachelor's degree in computer science from Central Michigan University.

Dedication: *To my lovely wife, Jodi, for all her insight. And to Terry Dennison, for showing me how to do it right by being a great mentor and friend.*

The Importance of Establishing a Strategy

Jack Barsky
Chief Information Officer
ConEdison Solutions

My Goals and Responsibilities

The fundamental goal of a chief information officer (CIO) is to provide vision and leadership to leverage information technology (IT) to attain competitive business advantage. There are three basic roles for IT in every modern company. First, there is the technology infrastructure, which includes such functions as e-mail, personal computing, network computing, internet access, and so on. Infrastructure is to a large degree commoditized, and it is the responsibility of the CIO to provide infrastructure services in a reliable and cost-effective manner. Second, there is the application support necessary to support the organizational functions of a modern corporation. These applications include, but are not limited to, human resource support, payroll, finance support, and so on. They tend to be rather similar across companies and across industries. Again, the CIO is responsible for providing this support in a reliable and cost-effective manner. The third aspect of IT is support for mission-critical core business functions. Here is where the CIO and the IT group can have a significant impact on revenue and the company bottom line.

As an example, for an energy services company that buys, sells, and trades electric commodity, knowledge and information are the most important assets. In fact, in a commodity business where no product changes hands and where the fundamentals of the business are all about the flow of data, certain functions of IT are not just supporting the business, they **are** the business. Competitive advantage for a commodity company is very much tied to how efficiently data is being processed and how effectively information is extracted from that data to enable the business to make informed decisions.

Finally, in today's day and age of real as well as cyber terrorism, a list of goals and responsibilities for a CIO cannot be complete without mentioning the requirement to secure the corporation's IT assets, protect them from outside threats, and be able to recover from a disaster.

The Art of Being a CIO

At first glance, IT appears to be as close to mathematics and hard science as any corporate function. After all, the binary system that is the foundation of modern IT is absolutely discreet. A bit is either on or off, there is no state in between. However, this close connection to mathematics does not imply that the IT realm should be managed in a technocratic fashion. On the contrary, the art of being a successful CIO centers primarily on the relationships between the technology groups and all other areas of the corporation. In a simplified model of technology delivery in a corporation, there are three components: the providers of technology services, the recipients of these services, and their interaction. The art of being a CIO is to understand and manage all three of these components.

First, there are the providers of technology services, the IT group itself. Traditionally, IT has attracted some of the best and brightest the job market has to offer. Those individuals share certain characteristics that must be well understood in order to effectively manage technology groups. For example, quite a few technicians enjoy the intellectual challenge inherent in their jobs so much that they would do the work regardless of compensation. On the other hand, their focus on creative solutions often takes on a perfectionist flavor that is almost never appropriate in our fast-paced corporate world that is forever impatient for technology solutions. The art of being a CIO requires a good understanding of the psyche of these individuals. This understanding is the necessary prerequisite to encourage, organize, and channel creativity with the aim to ultimately provide tangible value to the enterprise.

Second, the CIO needs to have a good understanding of the recipients of technology services. This requires a good grasp of the business, but at the more fundamental level of cognition, it requires an empathic ability to look at the world of technology from the viewpoint of the customers of technology. This leads directly to the third component in the technology delivery model, the interface between technology and the business. Good CIOs know how to speak the language of both groups and know how to successfully translate communication in both directions.

Misconceptions Surrounding the CIO

There are two prevalent misconceptions about the job of a CIO. The first is that being a CIO is primarily about managing technology. In spite of the fact that business schools, major trade publications, and many executives teach that the role of the CIO is business with a technology bent, this misconception has been quite persistent. It manifests itself clearly and directly in the widespread practice to promote highly capable technicians to managerial positions of ever-increasing responsibility. Unfortunately, most strong technicians are not very well equipped to handle the requirements inherent in a managerial job. In order to be successful, the CIO must be an ambassador of technology, a relationship builder, and an outstanding communicator. Therefore, this job requires a tremendous amount of emotional intelligence and self-awareness, which is not usually a strongpoint of technicians.

Interestingly, the second misconception is exactly the opposite of the first one, namely that IT can be run by somebody who has no foundation in technology. In my view, without an intuitive understanding of the value of IT, it is not possible to be an effective CIO.

Working Relationships with Other Executives

The ultimate goal of a public corporation is to maximize shareholder value, or in plain English, to make money. In every corporation, there are functions that are more central to that goal than others. In a simplified view, there are three basic functions important to the flow of money: revenue generation, cash collection, and accounting. In the energy supply industry, revenue is generated via the sale of creative and often complex commodity products that bear resemblance to financial instruments. Those products, once created and sold, require special processing at the back end. Therefore, in this business, a CIO must be closely aligned with the vice president of sales in order to provide competitive intelligence to the sales force and to support sales in the creation of new products. The second important executive an energy services CIO must be involved with is the vice president of operations. Billing and cash collection are crucial to the success of a commodity company. In the early stages of electric deregulation, many companies went bankrupt because they could not find a way to get accurate bills to their customers. In addition to complexity, billing is also subject to high volume. The proper application of IT will result in scalable automated solutions that are necessary to survive in a commodity business with slim gross margins. Finally, it is important for the CIO to be closely aligned with the chief financial officer. Proper accounting has always been important to a healthy corporation, but in light of recent stringent government regulations such as the Sarbanes-Oxley Act, this has become more important than ever. Industrial-strength systems solutions in support of proper accounting are not optional. In addition, all internal and external audits start with the flow of money, but since IT is so pervasive in the modern corporation, they quickly expand to include many IT functions.

The Skills Required of a Team Member

Character, most importantly integrity and team orientation, should precede any skills when considering someone for a team. Second to character is competence: members of a team must have a strong core competency in the area of their responsibility. For example, a director of database management and data warehousing must have a strong understanding of data management and architecture, just as the director of financial systems must know finance and the systems solutions to support this function. A good leader should also hire individuals that complement his or her own strengths and weaknesses. This requires a bit of self-knowledge and a great deal of courage to admit that one is not equally adept at every important function required for the job.

Two other skills are also important to qualify individuals to become members of an executive team. They are interpersonal and communications skills. The ability to interact with customers, peers, and subordinates in an effective manner is a fundamental prerequisite to a manager's success. A successful IT executive must also be able reduce the complexity of technology by speaking to his or her customers in plain business language.

Setting and Monitoring Team Goals

IT organizations should be methodical with regard to setting goals. A strategic approach requires a thorough understanding of the overall company strategy and a comprehensive business model. IT strategy should be well aligned with the business strategy and should be developed in close cooperation with the business leaders. The manifestation of this IT strategy should be a long-term strategic plan. This plan should be kept alive by making adjustments and additions (at least once a year) as dictated by changes in business direction.

The annual operational plan should be based on the strategic plan. Again, this plan should be determined in close cooperation with the business to assure optimal alignment. In order to monitor these goals, a company can institute a departmental scorecard system that tracks both the time and cost of projects, as well as the basic metrics agreed upon in various service level agreements that apply to day-to-day support of the business.

Advice for Team Members

Interestingly, most good and important advice falls in the category of common sense. For example, in our daily lives we constantly experience that things take longer and cost more than originally envisioned. How many do-it-yourself projects ever come in on time and on budget? The very same principle is at work when it comes to estimating resources for IT projects. Unlike many construction projects that have repeatable tasks, IT projects tend to be unique. Because of the complexity inherent in those projects, it is virtually impossible to know everything about the project at its very beginning. As projects are implemented, previously unknown information is discovered. The unknowns almost invariably break toward a negative outcome, which results in added cost and time.

The next piece of advice applies to individuals in all walks of life, but it is especially important to technology workers who are often unaware of the discrepancy between who they believe they are and how they are perceived by others. To others, we are the sum of the signals we are sending to the outside world. It is important that we are aware of these signals and align them as closely to the image we want to project. On the flipside of this coin, we find the word "empathy." It is much easier to understand others if we understand their frame of reference and their basic psychological makeup. Both empathy and aligning perception with reality go a long way in reducing miscommunication, which is most often the root cause for failure in IT organizations.

The Importance of IT strategy in Creating Success

A business-oriented strategy is vital for the long-term success of any IT organization. The very first step in any strategy must be the establishment of the right team. Even the greatest ideas become meaningless without capable arms, legs, and brains to translate those ideas into reality. Assembling the right team is fundamental and universal to all organizations in pursuit of a goal. The next layer in the strategic hierarchy is determined very much by situational factors. In IT terms, a successful strategy may focus on any one or multiples of the following:

- Implement a service-oriented architecture.
- Attain organization maturity and improve IT governance.
- Reduce cost.
- Run IT like a business.
- Outsource commodity-like functions to be able to focus on value-added IT services.
- Integrate major business applications to improve business work flow.

There are many other strategies that could be mentioned in this context, and each one of them could be valid and critical to the success of a given corporation. In my opinion, a good IT leader should not spend an inordinate amount of time to get strategies "just right." This may well result in analysis paralysis. Relentless execution is probably much more critical to ultimate success than getting strategies perfectly defined.

Difficult Situations

Throughout my career, difficult situations have almost never been about technology itself. Instead, they were associated with the challenge of managing technology and the people working with it. A common ailment to beset technology groups is the lack of structure and organization. As a result, those groups constantly operate in a reactive firefighting mode. Everybody works frantically, but nothing ever seems to get done. The interaction between IT and customers is fraught with broken promises, missed deadlines, and ultimately a deep distrust in the ability of IT to deliver. These kinds of challenges call for leadership and structure. Because of their individualistic tendencies, technicians often do not like to be subjected to a highly structured approach. However, there are ways to overcome this initial resistance. IT professionals are by nature very logical. If they are shown the logical connection between discipline and success, there will be enough buy-in for a start. As results start emerging, this buy-in will get stronger. Most individuals prefer to work in a group that delivers results and is well regarded by the rest of the company instead of constantly operating in firefighting mode, stressed out, and with no recognition from those they serve.

Difficult situations are relatively easy to handle, as long as one has control. However, much of the difficulty IT is faced with is associated with the interaction with its customers. Since IT pervades all facets of the modern corporation, it often becomes the focal point of all the politics of the entire organization. The demand for IT services is insatiable, but the resources to satisfy this demand are limited. It is arguably the most important job of a CIO to manage this very conflict. This is anything but a technology task. Rather, it requires diplomatic and teambuilding skills in an environment where one has very little control. A successful CIO is an executive who enables the leadership team to make collective decisions with regard to IT based on business priorities.

Overcoming Challenges

One of the most important challenges a CIO is faced with is communication. At the executive level and the level of his or her direct reports, the CIO has strong and direct influence over the quality of communication. However, there is very little direct control over the communication at the operational level where the work gets done. Miscommunication at that level is often the root cause of failure. Unfortunately, individuals with strong skills in technology often find clear and precise communication difficult.

There are several ways to address this issue and bridge the communication gap that may exist at all levels of the company. A CIO should lead by example; whenever there is a chance, he or she should allow individuals in the organization to be present during communication with business leaders. Direct reports should be involved in communication with top business leaders. At the operational level, it is important to promote individuals with communication skills into management positions. To further hone those skills, appropriate courses or programs such as Toastmasters and Carnegie should be employed. Finally and probably most importantly, a CIO should make sure all interaction with the business gets formalized and recorded in writing. Written communication requires individuals to be much more precise, which reduces the possibility of misunderstanding.

Another significant challenge is associated with perception management. The reality of a CIO is that technology tends to get noticed only when things break. For example, nobody ever seems to pay much attention to the marvelous combination of hardware and software that makes a personal computer work. However, the moment something malfunctions, the user gets upset. As a result, there is an inbuilt negative bias towards the ability of technology to deliver. One way to overcome this bias is to embrace the "Flying Fish Theory of Management." To illustrate this approach, imagine watching the surface of the ocean on a calm day, when there is little action. The moment a flying fish breaks through the surface and jumps up, everybody notices. In IT, the flying fish represents all occurrences that are outside of the norm. A manager has three ways of dealing with these "fish":

1. Anticipate the event and predict it.
2. Notice the event before anyone else and proactively explain it to the audience.
3. Have someone watch the ocean at all times and provide you with an alert and an explanation before anybody else is aware.

If these "fish" constantly surprise a CIO, it will be hard to convince the executive management team that everything is well under control in the IT world.

Expenses

My organization spends 60 percent of its budget on labor, 35 percent on hardware and software, and 5 percent on miscellaneous other expenses. In a company in which knowledge is the most important asset, this is an appropriate ratio. Because the business centers on data, any attempt to cut expenses in IT would hurt the business directly and immediately. Conversely, if additional moneys were to be available, I would spend it adding more creative talent to the team.

Research and Development

My company is not large enough to afford a dedicated research and development function in IT. Just because it is not institutionalized does not mean research and development does not take place. On the contrary, with the right individuals in the IT organization, research and development will take place by default. All associates are encouraged to contribute ideas on how to improve IT and its services to the company. I have always been an ardent supporter of what I call "creative play time," when individuals experiment with new approaches to arrive at creative and useful solutions. Obviously, such activities have to be channeled, but they should never be tightly supervised. To further nurture creativity, CIOs should be strongly supportive of training and education, and encourage active participation in professional organizations and technology user groups.

The History of the Deregulated Energy Industry

The deregulated energy business depends heavily on rules and mathematical models to function. Essentially, the foundation of this business is the use of financial instruments to manage the physical flow of energy and create efficiencies by introducing market-based competition in a previously monopolistic space. When deregulation was first attempted about a decade ago, everything was new and operating parameters for an energy service company would often change dramatically week by week. In such an environment, where the business model was a moving target, it was impossible to develop stable and mature IT support. As a result, the business had to be supported with spreadsheet-based solutions and some hastily assembled vendor packages. In those early days, survival of newly established companies often hinged on their ability to bill customers correctly and in a timely manner. Electric commodity bills for large industrial and commercial customers are much more complex than those for typical residential users. Most of the companies that were able to deploy automated solutions in support of complex billing are still thriving today. Many others, who did not succeed with this function, did not survive the fierce competition and had to cease operations.

Successful IT Strategies that Changed the Industry

Because of the early rapid changes and fluctuations in the deregulated energy business, it was essentially impossible to build a strategic IT architecture. Spreadsheets were gradually replaced with more industrial-strength systems, but those systems were essentially islands of information. Communication among those systems was mostly achieved via manual data entry. This type of insular IT was mirrored by the fact that business processes were neither optimal nor mature. Overall, this state of affairs provided significant obstacles to growth and exposed the entire industry, as well as each individual company, to tremendous risk via human error.

As the industry stabilized and processes became more predictable and repeatable, it became time for IT to take a more strategic approach and implement an enabling architecture. It was absolutely necessary to move away from the risky and non-scalable spreadsheet-based processes. The next step was to connect the existing islands of information in support of streamlined and well-designed back office procedures. This endeavor started with an in-depth analysis of the current state and the desired future state of the various business processes involved. The IT solutions were designed after the completion of the business analysis. As a result, my company now has an automated back office process that allowed us to significantly increase volume without having to add personnel on the operations side. In addition, the middleware-based technology solution allowed the business to quickly enter new commodity markets without incurring a huge startup cost. The entire middleware project, which was implemented in stages over a two-year period, is a great example of how IT can enable a business to grow and remain competitive.

Now that we are able to support the company main business line in an assembly-like fashion, it is important to go the next steps. In order to continue to support the business optimally, IT must make the transition from data processing to information to intelligence. "Information" is simply a state of affairs where business leaders are able to make informed decisions based on management reports. This analytical capability to dissect our whole portfolio and determine the profitability of individual products and customers is going to become more and more important in a business with ever-shrinking profit margins. "Intelligence" takes this concept to another level. By embedding business intelligence into our custom applications, we will be able to develop "what if" scenarios. Our business leaders will be able to simulate reality **before** it happens, rather than explaining things after the fact. For example, it is quite possible that targeting electricity customers with a certain usage profile may allow the company to significantly balance the wholesale portfolio and increase profitability, even if those retail sales result in a loss. At heart, commodity sales and trading is really synonymous with risk management. Energy services companies are paid by their customers to reduce their exposure caused by energy price volatility. There is an art to that management discipline, but to the extent we can introduce scientific analysis and quantify things, we can reduce this risk to a minimum and maximize profitability.

The Changing Role of the Technology Leader

Only about thirty years ago, CIOs were overseeing technology organizations where practically every initiative involved custom IT solutions to be built from scratch. Obviously, building such solutions took a long time, and as a result, IT exhibited relatively low productivity. Over the past thirty years, technology vendors would slowly emerge to sell basic infrastructure capabilities, operating systems, generic packages, and even specialized software solutions. The trend to buy solutions rather than build them is continuing. In addition, a strong push towards outsourcing more and more IT functions has added to the complexity of the area that is being overseen by today's CIO. Consequently, the role of the CIO has become much more demanding. In addition to the oversight of build activities, CIOs must infuse their organization with expertise in technology selection, vendor management, project management, contract management, and IT governance. As the number of technology alternatives has increased exponentially, so has the number of decisions to be made by the CIO. This clearly has increased, and will continue to increase, the responsibility of the CIO within the corporate landscape.

The future will bring even more daunting challenges for the modern CIO. The push by major vendors for computing on demand or "utility computing" will eventually create an entirely different globally connected IT space. Coupled with ever-increasing connectivity and bandwidth for the Internet, this will fundamentally change the way we all work. We will be connected to sources of information at all times, no matter where we are. This has tremendous potential for good, but it also carries the possibility for abuse. Managed correctly, this instant access to information will add a whole new dimension to the concept of freedom. Managed incorrectly, it may reduce individual freedom by tying people to their jobs at all times.

Two other things will be very important in this vast new information space: maintaining security and privacy, and finding a way of managing the tremendous amount of information to avoid complete overload. Both issues are already important today. We are really only at the beginning of the IT revolution, yet we already see those concerns taking shape. Even today, security is the most important concern when it comes to the Internet. Even today, a Web search can come up with hundreds, if not thousands, of items of information about a certain topic with little ability to filter and assess veracity. Future CIOs will have to manage these issues, but it is important that today's CIOs start thinking about them to assure that technology remains manageable and useful.

Jack Barsky is the chief information officer for ConEdison Solutions. In this role, he oversees all aspects of the company information technology infrastructure, ranging from management of day-to-day operations to setting strategic directions for information technology in a growing corporation.

In a career that spans two decades in information technology, Mr. Barsky has been with such companies as Metlife, United HealthCare, and Prudential Financial. He spent the early years of his career acquiring a hands-on foundation of information technology skills while working as application programmer, systems programmer, and database administrator.

During his information technology management career, Mr. Barsky held positions of increasing responsibility, including project manager, director for technology assessment, director of UNIX data center operations, and vice president of human resource systems. Before joining ConEdison Solutions, he was the chief operating officer for International Information Technology Team, an information technology consulting firm.

Mr. Barksy graduated as class valedictorian with a B.B.A. from Baruch College in 1983.

Technology: Changing the Way We Work

Lehi L. Mills

Chief Technology Officer

Travizon Inc.

Position Goals

To guide the company towards higher revenue, reduce expenses, and a faster return on investment on technology investments, and to increase customer and employee loyalty, company goals should include:

1. Distancing the company from competitors through better technology
2. Creating a tighter running operation by improving workflow through technology
3. Decreasing manual processes with intuitive technology
4. Creating customer loyalty through custom solutions

Moreover, by reducing expenses through automation, increasing revenues through technology, and creating an alternative revenue stream outside of a company's core competency with technology solutions, the company can move towards increasing revenue. In the case of global technology solutions, the chief technology officer (CTO) must be aware of each country's nuances as they seek to automate tasks and improve the flow of information between continents.

CTO Qualities for Success

Foremost, a CTO must be an innovative thinker. He or she must be able to understand what a customer is asking for and be able to create a viable solution. He or she must be intuitive and unafraid to act. He or she may go out on sales calls to meet with potential clients, as well as with existing customers, to gauge their requirements. Also, being aware of the competition and the products they offer may push the company to continue in different directions.

Challenges for the CTO

The first challenge is being able to deliver a solution in a timely manner that meets the customer's needs. Often, customers do not understand the complexity of creating a particular solution. This challenge can be overcome by setting the customer's expectations from the beginning on what the solution will and will not provide. Getting customers involved at the beginning of the product lifecycle helps define what the product will achieve, who the product is intended to help, what manual processes will be eliminated, and how long it will take to create the solution.

Another challenge is to keep the sales force tethered to what a solution can truly do, as opposed to what the customer is told, by training them on products and informing them of research and development plans.

Working Relationships

Working with the chief financial officer calls for an understanding and appreciation of cost management and increasing revenues. Sharing the same goals of reducing expenses and increasing revenues through the proper application of technology plants the seed for a powerful partnership.

The CTO may approach the vice president of sales in a different manner. Here, the creative ideas of what technology can achieve in theory are brought to the fore. When a choice between two disparate technologies is pending, the CTO might instruct the vice president on which solution will prove to be more effective as it applies to company goals and long-term growth strategy.

Team Goals

CTOs seek team members who can think independently and maintain their composure during stressful situations. Team members' goals are centered on three key areas:

1. Quality of service. Is the information presented to customers accurate?
2. Reduction of expenses. Are costs being controlled and operating expenses reduced?
3. Increase revenue. Employees are empowered and encouraged to come up with new innovations and ideas that can increase revenues.

A goal management system allows the company to reward and penalize employees depending on the outcome of a particular goal. For completing goals on time and within budget, employees can earn points that can be redeemed for gift certificates, extra time off, airline tickets, and much more. Penalties are assessed for poor performance, failing to complete assigned tasks, and overall quality of service. Some typical demerits can include a smaller percentage of a bonus, lower raises, and slower position advancement.

Team members also must listen to the customer and deliver a solution that exceeds their expectations. The team is meant to augment and improve customer service. It can be used to reduce expenses and increase revenues when applied correctly. Utilized effectively, it can create a better way of life for both customers and employees.

Strategizing

Going out on sales calls is the first step in a slump. Meeting with potential customers allows one to see what the competition is offering, as well as what the customer needs and what trends are. Getting customers to comment on showcased, new technology allows for the company to improve the usability of their services. When speaking with customers, the way they conduct their day-to-day business is always discussed. We discuss how their workflow operates between departments. Being able to sit with a customer and observe these processes as they take place allows us to identify and articulate solutions that will meet their need. Customers are the greatest resource to a company. Interacting with customers and seeing how they conduct business gives an edge in the market. If one develops products that are customer-centric, customers benefit. If one develops products that are technology-centric, technology benefits, but profits may take a hit.

A CTO must examine the scalability of every solution. If it solves a problem for one customer, it must solve the problem for others. When a new product is first developed, every piece of code written has been designed with the belief that it will last at least five years, and that it can easily adapt to a wide array of business situations. This allows the company to then resale single solutions on a global level to multiple customers.

Entering the global marketplace is another path to success; this entrance expands company vision and strategy with a whole new set of global solutions and products for customers that are typically larger in size. Global solutions are typically more complex, and require greater resources to complete on time. As such, a global solution should solve multiple business issues. Since a solution of this nature affects the entire enterprise as opposed to a regional division, there is a greater positive impact on the company. Such global solutions are often worth more to customers.

Big Money Spending

The biggest expense the information technology department incurs is salary, followed by software licensing, and then hardware purchases. Networks are a constant source of upkeep and improvement, and require monitoring around the clock. Reviewing future product and employee needs can guide the next phase of spending.

Mistakes and Misconceptions

The most difficult situation is often informing a customer that a request cannot be completed. As the needs of a customer can be so finite that the scalability of the solution is lost, the customer must bear the burden of paying the costs. The CTO must broker a solution and compromise.

The biggest misconception about the CTO position is that a CTO is technically but not business savvy. It is untrue, however, that one who is technically oriented only cares about technology, and has no vision or desire for the growth of the business.

The CTO: Past and Future

Technology changes rapidly, and thus the CTO must be continually innovating. By aligning with the right partners and customers, and specifically by meeting with current and potential customers on a regular basis, a company is kept abreast of both competitors and customer needs.

Technology will continue to change and become more invisible to the average person. As radio frequency identification improves and becomes more mainstream, great leaps will be made in delivering real-time information to corporations.

Three Golden Rules

Dare to dream big. We're currently bidding on a piece of business that is eight times larger than our largest customer. In order to compete in this arena, we have pushed our technology beyond that of our most advanced rival, and have created several innovative solutions along the way.

Deliver solutions to your customers that solve their problems, not add to them. A university on the West Coast that had struggled managing the logistics for their sports teams asked us for help. After observing how they had historically managed this process, we put together a Web-based solution that would not only help the travel arrangers, but also the coaches of each unit. Since most of these coaches didn't have time to go out to the Internet and manage their team travel, we devised several processes that "pushed" the information directly to the coaches via e-mail, PDA, and cell phone.

Be fiscally responsible. Technology drives our company, our growth, and our distinction. With the technology being this important in the day-to-day operation, it would be easy to push for larger budgets and ask for less control on spend. But this is exactly how most companies get in trouble. A CTO must have the self-restraint to operate within a budget, and more importantly, look at creative alternatives that will reduce expenses. This could include outsourcing labor where necessary or opting not to purchase big-ticket items.

Lehi L. Mills has copyrighted three software technologies with the United States Library of Congress. Prior to working for Travizon, he was the director of research and development instrumental in pioneering advanced reporting techniques in the corporate travel industry. Currently, he is working on digital DNA algorithms as they apply to the underlying architecture of corporations and their profitability.

Mr. Mills has been featured in several industry magazines regarding new technologies created for the travel industry.

Helping Companies Accomplish More

Julie F. Butcher

Vice President, Information Technology

MDC Holdings Inc.

The Functionality of Technology Management

Technology management involves the maintenance of existing technology systems. In my situation, that management includes everything from the telephone systems to the copy machines. With systems and equipment running as designed, the business operations supported continue to produce results without interruption. By planning for the future and participating new technology opportunities, technology managers join with the business teams to make operational units more effective year over year. Technology managers act as consultants to determine where future technological capabilities will be of greatest use to the business.

The goal of technology management is to analyze technology opportunities that allow company employees to accomplish more. Those technology opportunities include everything from PDA devices to high-powered computing equipment, and business application systems to cellular telephones. The important thing is to determine which of these devices or applications truly increase productivity and which are just fun to own and cool to use.

Being a Successful Technology Leader

The ability to communicate is the integral part of being a technology leader. Through written and verbal communication, a technology leader must be able to translate highly technical concepts into information the business can understand and act upon. Technology leaders require the ability to turn massive amounts of data into usable intelligence. Experience with technology enables these leaders to understand new technological opportunities. As a result, they can distinguish between devices that will move the business forward technically.

Being a technology leader requires a combination of leadership skills and technical knowledge. He or she must also have knowledge of both technology and of business, as well as how the two aspects intersect. As a result, a technology leader is liaison between highly technical individuals and the less technical business staff of an organization.

The successful technology leader requires a defined vision and the effective use of personal intuition. Most technical teams desire technical leaders. To lead them effectively, a technology leader must maintain a technical vision that he or she articulates frequently. In my humble opinion, an individual's internal voice or intuition is formed from experience, aptitude, and knowing right from wrong. I encourage my teams to listen to that internal voice. If it doesn't "feel" right, it probably isn't right.

By watching other leaders, an individual can emulate what to do and what **not** to do. A leader must also be willing to seek ideas or advice from their teams, and then be willing to act on those ideas. Giving credit to others does not diminish your own contributions and ideals.

Overcoming the Challenges of a Technology Leader

One of the greatest challenges for a technology leader is continually expressing to the business how much technology can improve business operations. For the executives who do not understand technology, they view it as potentially wasteful spending, especially when the business is doing well. The challenge is making executives understand the technology enough to see its benefits by explaining it in a clear and non-technical way. The more technical the subject, the more non-technical explanation is required. A smaller, more frequent dose of information on technical topics is often a more effective way to communicate the necessary information to the business.

In a world where experienced resources possessing just the right skill set are difficult to find, I choose to overcome the challenge of finding the technical resource with the exact experience by finding people who possess attitude and aptitude. I have found that some companies search for individuals with very specific technology skills to match the technology of their particular business. While technical skills are certainly important, a candidate's aptitude and attitude can play a larger role. An individual needs the aptitude to acquire new skills and understand new technologies. Attitude is the second required piece. The appropriate attitude is one of energy and passion and desire to do those extracurricular activities that build stronger skill sets.

Successful Strategies

The number-one strategy for building a solid technical team is diversity. Diversity in technical skill sets, communication skills, and customer orientation can mix to create a team capable of managing a myriad of situations. In building a team with a diverse skill set, it is important that each member of the team possess a good understanding of the value that is found in skills that may not be their own.

The attention to and development of influence is another successful strategy. Technical managers should spend time meeting with customers, peers, and employees to develop a level of trust that leads to the ability to influence others. Influence of company leaders is also important. Technical managers should make every effort to know their own leaders, the motivations of their leaders, and the overall objectives of their leaders. By maintaining personal contact and relationships with these individuals, technology leaders develop the ability to influence them in business and technical decisions.

Also key to success is the true appreciation of others' contributions to the business and the technology. A leader must clearly and often appreciate the work others do and recognize their contributions to the success of the team. The giving and receiving of feedback should be considered a gift. My teams are encouraged to accept feedback as if it were a gift. Like a gift, with feedback you get to decide exactly how to use it, or if you choose to use it at all. Viewing feedback, positive or negative, as a gift makes it easier to accept, review, and implement where desired.

Technology managers must continually review new technical strategies and their potential applications to the business. With a good understanding of the business needs and the "futures" of technology, technology managers become trusted advisors and more than just the "IT guys." Technologists are curious by nature and are anxious to discover and research new technology. That curiosity has the opportunity to provide innovation options for the business.

Working with Other Executives

In our organization, technology leaders work closely with the chief financial officer and the head of the treasury organization to fund information technology (IT) initiatives. Those initiatives are usually in support of an operational unit's technical needs, but can also include IT infrastructure and productivity tools. Once project requests emerge from an IT organization partnering with the business, the chief information officer (CIO) presents the project to an executive steering committee. In these presentations, there is generally little discussion of the underlying technology, but rather discussions of the financing required to implement the technology, and most importantly, the benefits to the corporation to be gained through the implementation of the technology.

These leaders also maintain frequent communication with CIOs and chief technology officers (CTOs) of other companies. The homebuilding industry is very open to sharing technology information. These discussions allow the industry to use the experience of others to make better technical choices and to ensure the success of IT projects. As a technical leader, having a sounding board that is experiencing many of the same challenges has allowed us to make better choices and increased the probability of success in our technical endeavors.

Setting Successful Goals

High-level IT goals begin with synchronizing business goals and the technology to support the business goals. From an IT perspective, a technology leader must tailor the IT goals to the business needs of the company. Key goals for our IT organization for this year include focusing on people—their development, their challenging assignments and recognition of contributions, technology leadership in the homebuilding space, exceptional service, and exceptional product delivery. Each employee from help desk staff, to desktop servers, to development staff, to business analysts has documented, supporting goals that then fit into the broader organizational goals.

Each individual's goals are determined, and measurements are defined to document the success of the goals early in the year. Those objectives are reviewed, results are documented, and necessary adjustments are made on a quarterly basis. Success can also come in the more personal form of achieving the three golden rules of being a technology leader—partnering with business, building a good team, and staying ahead of the curve.

Advice from a CIO

I give the same advice to new leaders or to people who have been leading teams for years. That advice is:

Provide a challenging work environment and assignments that allow people to continue to learn. Compensate your employees fairly. And plan the work accordingly to ensure that team members have time to spend in activities outside of work.

I encourage my leaders and their team members to say please and thank you, two simple phrases that are completely underutilized in corporate America. It never ceases to amaze me what effect the words "thank you" can have on a team and the morale of an individual.

If it doesn't "feel" right, it probably isn't right. I encourage employees to use their instincts and intuition to make decisions as much as they use the supporting data.

A long time ago, a manager told me that if I took care of the company, the company would take care of me. While stages of downsizing cloud this principle, it remains true at its core. If the decisions individuals make are more focused on the company than on themselves, the company will grow and in turn provide continued opportunities for its employees.

Combating the Expenses, Challenges, and Misconceptions of a Technology Team

The largest expense for most technology teams is providing ongoing support for existing technical platforms. By working closely with business teams, technical teams can determine the best way to spend those ongoing support dollars to maintain a stable technical environment, but also find ways to move the business forward.

In addition to managing those ongoing support expenses, a challenge for any IT is meeting the ever-present demand of the business to help their employees become more productive. Garnering participation of the business in the definition of requirements, vendor tools selections, or product development is often difficult because the business teams already have full-time jobs doing other things. IT projects are never as successful as they could be without participation of the business. It is so important that key business team members be given the time to participate, in detail, on IT projects that will increase the productivity of the business.

One misconception of the life of a CIO is that they are continually handling those lofty technical issues. Today's CIO handles the small things like malfunctioning cell phones and video conferencing microphones that fail to work when needed. He or she does not spend every day researching or working with high-level technology or hobnobbing with the other executives, but instead deals with some of the lowest-level technical issues facing the business. IT professionals are responsible for most anything that has a keyboard, touchtone, or cord. These misconceptions are frequent because there is limited understanding of technology in the business world.

Top Resources

Many CIOs utilize technology or industry publications such as *CIO Magazine* or Gartner and Forrester research for trends and common sense information. Leadership books are helpful, too. Because technologists are curious by nature, an open environment exists in which other individuals discuss new ideas. By voicing these ideas, team members become resources in themselves. Other resources include experts in specialized technologies. Some of my most used, best advisors are the members of my team. They each possess technical specialties, and their diverse backgrounds provide analysis of problems from so many different angles.

Identifying Future Changes

Technology is becoming more and more a partner to business. Business leaders are more often acknowledging the role technology can play in reducing costs and increasing profitability, and using the CIO to discuss those options.

In the future, technology leaders, along with the business, will decide which technology skills should be maintained and developed in-house and which skills or services should be bought from other organizations. Each company must determine where its business value lies within a technology organization. The pendulum will continue to swing from outsourcing to insourcing until companies that truly provide outsourcing provide the same level of service an internal organization can provide.

Largely, these changes should not effect the way an IT organization operates. The technology leader must still provide motivation for employees and the analysis that different technology options provide.

Julie Butcher is vice president of information technology at MDC Holdings Inc. MDC is the parent of several companies supporting building and sales of Richmond American Homes. She leads a team of more than 140 technology professionals providing information technology services and support to MDC.

Butcher has twenty-five years in the technology industry, half of which was spent as a consultant for EDS, where she led technology projects for General Motors, Baxter Diagnostics, Hughes Offshore, Dow Chemical, and other companies, large and small. She has also held senior management positions with EchoStar Communications (The Dish Network), Coors Brewing Company, Level 3 Communications, and AT&T Broadband.

Dedication: *To my wonderful family: Parke, Rachelle, Alex, and KC, and to my loving and beloved parents who have supported me always.*

Creating Strategic Momentum

Ric Villarreal

Senior Vice President and Chief Information Officer

Oakwood Worldwide

sful Technology Leader

...y goal is to create strategic momentum for technology and business innovation. My position is about facilitating the strategic goals of the company. I am a member of the executive committee; I sit on the board. I provide insight and support when implementing high-value initiatives with all the division heads. I also provide an initiative prioritization process to look for that executive commitment.

Being a technology leader is about creating an environment in which our internal customers have an absolute need to include the information technology (IT) perspective in problem solving with opportunities they may have within their business operation. A chief information officer (CIO) needs to have as much credibility as a business executive, as we do as a technologist. Executive leaders need to understand that we have the same goals and that we understand their challenges as business leaders. Of course on the technology side, we need to be seen as innovative technologists and futurists.

Developing the program management office (PMO) has been a successful strategy for me. A company our size, with our aggressive growth and migration strategies, needs to have the PMO pervasive in every project, whether a technology project or business initiative. One of the key elements for a successful PMO is an executive steering committee, made up of all the divisional heads. The bimonthly meeting gives a great deal of exposure and support to every initiative. The executives each present their initiatives and the current status to the group, including the chairman of the board.

The idea of centralizing our key business processes is another strategy I have used. We used to have our field offices around the country do their own billing, accounts receivable, and collecting. We also had a completely decentralized reservation system. Today, we have centralized accounts receivable, accounts payable, and have established the first phase of a centralized reservation system. Centralization provides specialization and a consistent implementation of process improvement, as well as very effective checks and balances. We are looking for more opportunities in customer service and in the reservation process. These strategies have made a direct impact on the bottom line.

If I could offer up the golden rules for being a technology leader, I would say that those in technology leadership need to feel that they are solving business problems or facilitating business opportunities. Not just solving technology problems. If everyone in the IT organization shares this perspective with our internal customers, we all focus on the components that will ultimately help us reach our strategic goals. You also need to hire great people. Problem solvers that rally the team to gang up on a problem. You have to hire people who are smarter than you are and who can infect other people with their great attitude and perspective.

The best piece of advice I've ever received from another technology leader is to focus on high-value initiatives. Maintain high executive commitment and ensure that adequate, and maybe even backup, resources are aligned to guarantee success.

Challenges

The corporate housing industry is different from the hospitality hotel industry we are all familiar with. Like a hotel, we have some fixed inventory of apartments in Oakwood buildings, but most of the apartments our guests stay in are from our virtual apartment inventory. We lease apartments in areas where our clients want to stay, we furnish them, decorate them, and turn on the utilities, and our corporate guests can then move into their home away from home for thirty days or more. Of course, the biggest challenge is managing that virtual inventory. Knowing how many apartment units to lease, for how long, and in what geographic area, while trying to minimize how long an apartment is empty. We are paying rent, and not collecting revenue. Because Oakwood is worldwide, we have this challenge in every major market in the world. In markets where apartment inventory is tight, we lease a core number of units in desirable cities on long-term leases to ensure we lease a minimum number of apartment units available for our customers' needs.

Another challenge we have is taking the needs of the business, our strategic goals versus technical goals such as migration. When we develop our business strategy, we need to blend the business priority with our technology priority. There needs to be a clear understanding that our technology strategy will enable our business strategies in the future.

I think one of the most difficult situations is when an executive sponsor starts to point fingers when an initiative has issues. It means an executive does not have the ownership or accountability for a project. Sometimes, it's because the executive is just intimidated by the process or it's not progressing the way they thought, or they are getting into details they may not understand. The most effective thing I can do is to over-communicate the competency of the project and reset expectations.

Overall, the biggest misconception about IT is that we think about nothing but spending big money on solutions. I think this gap will always exist to some point. Even though the return on investment may be there, robust, well-architected, scalable solutions always seem to cost much more than they should. After all, once you pay hundreds of thousands of dollars for the software, all you get is a few CDs or a five-minute download. That doesn't look like a million dollars.

Changes in Technology Leadership

Technology leadership has shifted and continues to shift from a back-of-the house information services department to being part of the business drive and strategy. The more we involve ourselves in being part of business solutions and having a broader perspective of the business, the more I think we'll attract broader businessmen with technology backgrounds to the field. This will lead to more and more technology leaders as presidents and chief executive officers.

Working Relationships

I work most closely with the heads of all our divisions and the chief financial officer. I need to understand their working environment, as well as their long-term goals. What do they need to react to on a day-to-day basis? How have their priorities changed during the year? When I have a good understanding of their short- and long-term priorities, and what changes them, I can help either influence or facilitate that path.

For example, the Oakwood Corporate Housing division that manages our non-Oakwood building inventory needed a reservation system. Unlike a hotel with its fixed unit inventory, a virtual inventory business model presents some very complex challenges when it comes to designing a reservation system. My detailed knowledge of these business processes has enabled me to support the executive sponsor throughout the design and implementation of our new reservations system.

My Team

Because I am part of the executive group, I often get the opportunity to explain my team's roles in the entire process. It's repetitive. It's important for me to continually communicate the process and the value it will bring to the final product. There are many times the project management overhead is perceived as "overkill" by executive sponsors.

My team members need to be accountable; they need to know what part of the process they own in delivering on final product. We are looking for team members with strong practiced methodology and the ability to tune the process when necessary.

The goals for the project are set using milestones, both budgetary and timeline-based, to meet the needs of the customer. Accountability comes through frequent PMO and steering committee meetings, and is tied back to incentives. The advice I find myself giving my team most often is to understand the customer's requirements and set very clear expectations. Good, clear expectations help avoid panic and distractions.

Utilizing Key Resources

We have a budget allotment for forward-looking projects, called the "dream team." This team looks forward in hardware technology, telecommunications technology, and tools for developing and tracking project management. They present new things that are coming on board to the rest of the team. From time to time, we take the next step and build prototypes or lab test new concepts. It's not about staying ahead in our use of technology; it's about having the best fit technology available when we need it. It's more important to maintain cutting-edge knowledge.

I think analytical resources are useful in my position and in this marketplace. I play a role in validating business challenges, so when an executive has a business challenge, I have access to all the information. It's important for me to sit down with the analysts and understand the issues to validate the situation as a business opportunity. I find that strong business and financial analysts have been great resources for us, as are the business intelligence tools we use.

Team Expenses

The biggest expenses for our team involve consulting. It's a decision left to the team leaders. I don't want anyone to believe that all good ideas have to come from within the team. Sometimes, the best idea is to bring someone in from the outside to offer an objective and/or specialized point of view. Once the team gets another perspective, we expect them to build on what they have learned. There is a difference between jumping to consultants for every issue and using consultants to augment our team's experience and brain trust.

As Oakwood Worldwide's senior vice president and chief information officer, Ric Villarreal directs the strategic implementation of key programs and initiatives that make up the platform enabling Oakwood's plans for aggressive growth. Villarreal also leads Oakwood's information technology team as the chief information officer, and is responsible for its technology strategy, which includes the migration from its twenty-year-old legacy environment to a leading-edge .NET platform.

Some of Mr. Villarreal's most notable initiatives include implementation of a thin client architecture, which has saved Oakwood millions in PC support and maintenance since its deployment. This has allowed Oakwood to implement a migration and integration platform. The platform has given Oakwood the ability to implement off-the-shelf software applications, and the ability to integrate with most any customer's automated processes.

Mr. Villarreal joined Oakwood in 1997 as the director of process engineering, championing a new direction of business processes for Oakwood Corporate Housing, Oakwood's third-party corporate housing division. He currently directs a staff of forty-six in the information systems department and the program management office.

Mr. Villarreal's latest project for Oakwood Worldwide has been to complete a Siebel sales and call center implementation, and his team was able to do so in less than four months.

Prior to Oakwood, Mr. Villarreal had a successful sixteen-year tenure at Xerox Corporation, where he worked in various capacities within the printing and copier divisions during their heyday. Villarreal was a call center manager, account executive, and director of training and video productions. He oversaw one of the first total quality management design teams that earned Xerox the Malcom Baldrige Award.

Mr. Villarreal is a certified process engineer and is certified in total quality management. He participates on the advisory board of several Fortune 100 companies, and is an active member of the National Management Association.

He currently resides in Los Feliz, California with his wife, and is the proud father of two sons and a grandfather of two.

Setting the Vision and Delivering on the Goals

Steve Hannah

Vice President and Chief Information Officer
CRST International

Business Goals

Our technology goals are aligned with the biggest needs of the business. The first goal is to remain focused on the key projects the internal business customers need to have completed, and to complete them on time so the business objectives and plans keep moving at the expected pace. How do we measure if we're being successful in that regard? A very common saying is, "If you can't measure it, you cannot fix it." So a series of technology metrics were defined and published via dashboards that tell us whether or not we're improving and how we're servicing the customer. One of those metrics is an on-time delivery of our projects. More than 80 percent of the time, when we say a project is going to be completed by a certain date, it is completed. That builds credibility, trust, appreciation, and respect. It also focuses us on the proper resources and allocation assignments of our staff. Currently, the team is executing at an 85 percent-plus service rating for on-time delivery to the customer. A key factor in the success of this goal is a strong emphasis on project lifecycle planning. This process, properly implemented, ensures that proper scope, analysis, communication, development, testing, and implementation measures are followed during the life of the project.

The second goal is to reduce the number of hours spent on rework due to errors and misunderstanding of the customer's request. Time spent reworking a project due to errors is lost time and does not serve the needs of the customer. It only frustrates all parties involved. It is our goal that less than 1 percent of the technology team's completed hours be attributable to an error rate. Customer satisfaction has to be a key benchmark of any technology team. My customers are internal, and they have to be satisfied with the results they're getting from the technology team. We can be replaced, so we have to continue to earn our stay every day. My team has been able to earn high customer ratings on our service, solutions, and communications due to a strong work ethic and passion about what we do. The third key goal is the amount of time a project request will rest on the backlog list before staff resources are available to meet the need. The key element in this area is to make sure you have a defined process to request projects and a good understanding of the talent on your team, a focus on completing projects the first time, and a strong acceptance of accountability for completing the projects within the defined scope of hours. By following the project lifecycle planning process and focusing on the items listed above, together we have been able to reduce the backlog request by 62 percent, thus improving the reputation of the technology team and the service to our business customers. Other metrics we watch closely are: application availability, downtime performance, financial budget performance, total cost of ownership, and continuous learning of the technology team.

The first goal focuses on how we are conducting ourselves as an information technology (IT) team in responding to the requests of the business. The second goal involves putting in place a deployment and integration plan that will help us effectively use data information and move the company to a leadership position. The third goal is about putting the infrastructure in place. We want to build and cultivate partnerships throughout the business. Technology departments cannot be an island; we cannot be successful by ourselves. We can only be successful with support and relationships from around the business. We strongly encourage our teams to get out of their offices and meet with the business in order to achieve success. We also strive to create an environment of continuous learning. As technologist, we ought to be the agents of change—if we're not continuously learning, how can we bring the changes necessary for the business? Another way of looking at it is if we truly have passion about what we do, a person should have a deep desire to keep learning and staying fresh on the area of technology that is served.

Strategies for Achieving Success

I am charged with the responsibility of creating a strategy to ensure that our systems are available: they're up, they're available, they're running efficiently, and people can use the systems and solutions we provide. The second strategy is making sure the business processes we follow are as streamlined and error-free as possible. This comes down to mapping out the business process currently being followed and determining the manual labor steps, along with where the opportunities for errors exist within the process. We then design a technology solution that will hopefully reduce the number of manual steps, and put checks and balances in place to reduce opportunity for errors. A key strategy step for success is ensuring that the technology we're implementing has a foundation built on industry standards. If a technology organization is bringing in a lot of diverse technology, the support and training costs associated are going to rise due to integration issues and staff resource allocation. With the key infrastructure layers defined via standards, one can reduce the cost of ownership and the amount of development time it takes to integrate other systems.

A key priority is to make efficient use of all the data information you obtain in order to understand trends, so business intelligence and electronic dashboards can be effective for the business. There are four different stages to understand when managing the information flow of a business. The first stage is data, which consists of pieces of information that are not related to each other. When you start taking pieces of data and relating them to each other, you bring information together. With information in hand, the businessperson can transform it into knowledge. Knowledge of the business and its customers can be mined into dollars. I am a firm believer that databases, properly designed, should inform the business of issues and opportunities instead of the user having to wait for a report or run a query. Our investment and growth in technology capabilities today should make this a common strategy of the business. When working with our systems, I try to determine how I can turn that knowledge into dollars—either saved dollars or increased revenue dollars. Another key strategy that many people follow, including myself, is to look for ways to consolidate technology to lower the total cost of ownership and improve the service and business continuity planning process. The range of opportunity in this case starts with server consolidation up to and including data center consolidation. In many companies, you have multiple computer centers that add significant costs and can cause problems in disaster recovery opportunities. Always look for ways to consolidate those and bring them in line with standards, thus improving your opportunity to better serve the business in a problem situation and lower your total cost of ownership in the process.

Be a Business Partner

Spend as little time as possible in your office. In order to understand the issues the business is facing, you must get out of your office and spend time with key business managers to understand how technology might be able to help in the process. However, it is very important that when you do meet with the business managers, do not speak as a technologist, but communicate as a business partner. Learn the language the business speaks and realize that most businesspeople are not impressed with the acronyms that are so common in technology world. Use this valuable time to find out what the key issues are, educate others on the value of technology, and then motivate your staff to deliver the best products and services possible. Success in this process does not have as much to do with technology—it's about being a business partner and establishing relationships.

A key skill in being successful is being a good listener so you can understand what the customer is telling you, and also what they're not telling you. Many times, this is a skill that needs to be developed and continuously worked on. Realize that it is more important to hear and understand what the other person is telling you so you can then design the proper solution to meet their needs. Technology leaders must have the ability to think strategically and communicate a vision for technology; they need to be held accountable for the technology vision and make sure it is aligned with the business. Technology leaders should be strategic thinkers rather than always focusing on the tactical side. We must have the ability to look at the big picture and then create a strategy that solves the whole problem, not just one piece of it. The ability for technology leaders to have a strong awareness of business and understand what the business does is growing at a fast rate today. A strong technologist who does not understand the business and does not have an established reputation as a business partner is going to be left behind. Understand the issues the business faces. Understand the balance sheet. Financial knowledge is important, along with the ability to measure progress. Technology leaders should be able to communicate both one on one and one on many. The ability to inspire others and model a commitment to quality service is key.

Utilizing Research and Resources

In my group, we have a stated goal to be a team focused on continuous learning; research and development should be a normal process within the workday. Research and development are done via many avenues, such as reading, conferences, formal training, Web research, and so on. Ideas are formulated and proven via prototypes. We use prototypes to show the business what can be done before the investment of development and systems are made. My team puts together a prototype (anything from a PowerPoint presentation to an application that shows functionality) so the company can measure the value before we launch an opportunity. The prototype process helps build interest, partnerships, and get people to understand the value of technology and see what you will be getting before you "buy it."

I utilize outside resources by talking with others who have my same job function, so I can share their knowledge. I also have a lengthy reading list of magazines and books on leadership, business, and technology. In addition, I look at comparable metrics to gauge the success of my team and how we can raise the bar to become a high-performance team. Targeted conferences on technology and business leadership are helpful, as are mentors. I have two mentors: one professional mentor and one personal mentor. I have the ability to be honest and say I screwed up, and get advice on how to handle a situation. I learn, observe, and measure resources, and I try to apply those lessons to my own situation.

From the resource perspective, our biggest expenses are in the areas of staffing, hardware, communication, and disaster recovery. Budgeting money for these areas depends on how they align with the goals of the company. If spending requests are not supported by a goal or objective, they most likely won't happen. Also, a return on investment should be conducted on an expense to make sure it's a sound business decision. Money is a finite resource. If I take the approach of investing in technology for the sake of it being "cool"—but it doesn't bring business value—I'm not doing my job.

Planning and Tracking Progress

Transportation is the industry I operate within; we are a trucking company that meets the needs of many types of customers. All of the revenue-making assets are mobile. We communicate with drivers via satellite communications, but the logistics of communicating with your mobile trucks and drivers in a time-sensitive business make the process very interesting and exciting.

We put a strong emphasis on project planning. In my experience, some projects are failures because the necessary planning was not done up front, and the team did not really know what business problem they were trying to solve. Larger projects of course have a more formal approach to project planning, but even the smallest project should have certain elements of

planning and communication involved to increase the oppc
success. It's about life cycle management; you don't install tech
leave it alone. You need to manage it and understand when it is no longer
meeting the needs of the business, whether it's a piece of hardware or
software. Everything has a defined life. If you can't measure something, you
can't fix it, and if you try to, most likely you will make it worse. I use
dashboards and metrics to track the progress of changes we're implementing,
as well as our own performance. This proven methodology provides high
visibility of projects—our project list is open to anyone in the company. We
celebrate our wins, acknowledge our losses, and try to be an open book in
that regard. We also focus on being partners with the business; we don't want
to be the technology geeks, we want to be motivated people who bring an
understanding of how technology can be applied to business problems. In my
view, that is bringing value to the business.

Technology Leader Challenges

One of the biggest challenges is the fast pace of changing technology. I do
my best to stay ahead of this challenge by maintaining a long reading list.
But, I understand that I can't be an expert in everything, so I focus on
making sure I have good people around me who I can learn from and
depend on. Having the right team in place is a key element of success. In
most technology organizations I have been involved with, we did not have
the luxury of "B" and "C" players. Due to staffing limitations, we have to
have "A" players and bring our best game everyday.

One of the biggest areas of value for me as leader of technology is a
technology peer group. These groups consist of people with similar jobs,
perhaps in different industries, who can share with me their experience on
what's working and what's not. Finding the right groups to be a part of can
save a great deal of time and money, not to mention the ability to quickly
send an e-mail requesting information from others on the priority topic the
chief executive officer has just raised.

Working on projects you know are going to reduce the workforce is a huge
challenge. We're talking about families and real people—that can be both
mentally and emotionally grueling. It is important to stay focused on the

)usiness needs and why we're here: to bring technology solutions to make the business more competitive.

One of the most difficult situations you can be faced with is justifying the replacement of legacy technology that may be a key foundation, but the replacement of which does not have a proven return on investment. Some technology isn't necessarily going to bring more customers or save the company money, but it's a foundation layer to the business. I work to overcome that challenge by doing a lot of research, planning, and communicating of the need early in the process. I try to make sure the business is aware early in the process of what the need is, and put together a strong presentation on the reliance and dependency we have on this particular layer as a business. It helps to bring an established history of success in determining the priority of previous projects, so your credibility is high when you say that a particular function needs to be replaced.

An additional challenge is educating the business on technology. This involves not just the features on the software, but also the continuous education that must occur to get the most out of an investment. I look for ways to communicate and educate in anything we do. This can be done via newsletter, intranets, scheduled "lunch and learns," one-on-one time, e-mail footers, and formalized classes, just to name a few.

The biggest misconception about my position is that I'm a master of all aspects of technology. I'm not, but that idea exists because my title says I am. Some people also think I'm more technology-focused than business-focused. I used to be, but most of the things I deal with now are business issues and problems not necessarily solely related to technology. These misconceptions exist because my area of influence is technology-based, but these misconceptions are overcome with time, communication, and earning the right to be viewed as a business partner.

Keeping Everyone in Step

I work closely with the chief executive officer, to whom I report directly. I also work with the chief financial officer, the presidents of each division (four different divisions within our company), and the vice president of business development. I need to know the issues they're dealing with on a daily basis. What are the outside factors that can affect their businesses? What drives them (what motivates them, what kind of people are they)? What are the measurements they use to determine success (so we can make sure we have common ground)? I also want to know their views of technology—does it add value, or is it just a cost?

My group exists to provide the most efficient technology solutions, based on industry standards, that meet or exceed the needs of our customers. As a group, we focus on being good business partners by creating a continuous learning environment, utilizing best practices via cycle planning, and delivering a high level of service to our customers.

An important lesson to learn is that everyone will not march to the same beat of the drum you march to. It's important to look back and make sure people are with you. My job is to keep everyone in step. As a technology leader, it's easy to get caught up in the excitement of the technology. There comes a time in your career where you have to put the screwdriver and programming template away and focus on developing others and providing the vision to direct the staff on where we are going. My job is not to implement the technology myself, but to define the vision, the roadmap, and to inspire and motivate others to success.

Working as a Team

The most important skills I'm looking for in team members have little to do with technology; I can teach technology. I'm looking for passion: do you really love what you do? When it becomes a *job*, something's wrong. I look for a person with a focus on customer service and a strong desire to deliver the best possible results to the customer. Treat the customer the way you like to be treated. A strong work ethic is essential—if you're the type of person I have to manage, you will not be successful on my team. Finally, the desire to work as a team is necessary. I'm not interested in superstars; I'm interested in people who want to win, and lose, as a team.

Strategic planning for technology helps us identify the key issues and properly set our goals and objectives for the coming year. At a minimum of an annual basis, we go through a technology strategic planning process that helps us make sure our priorities are in alignment with the goals of the company. You never want to have a goal for your group that doesn't match the goals the company sets; if that happens, you're probably setting yourself up for failure. We go through a "SWOT" analysis that helps us determine our strengths, weaknesses, opportunities, and threats. The goals we set are part of an effort to move the weaknesses to strengths, take advantage of our existing strengths, and neutralize threats, while trying to seize any opportunities that make good business sense. If the business wants to do something, and it requires knowledge in a particular area of technology we don't have, that's a weakness.

We have implemented personal and team-based key performance indicators. In some cases, the dashboards we use help give us the measurements of those key performance indicators. The managers have one-on-one meetings with their direct reports, and then they have meetings with me to ensure that the communication on needs and issues are out there. We do a lot of reporting on the company's goals and objectives, and how technology is playing a positive or negative role in each of them.

I give my team advice on dealing with customers who may or may not know what they really want. I also give advice on communicating with people outside of the technology group in a business format, to ensure that we're not communicating in megabytes; we should be translating our knowledge into the language of the business, so people don't turn us off. Mostly my advice centers around ensuring that we are looking out for the best interests of the company and ensuring that we have exhausted all possible efforts to meet the customer needs efficiently.

IT: Past and Future

Currently, there is a lot more accountability to the business and the board of directors than ever before. Skills inventories and continuous learning are playing larger roles. These days, it's so easy to become obsolete in skill sets. It's getting harder to cost-justify technology changes. In many cases, a significant part of the savings technology can bring has already been realized, and the open checkbook concept of preparing for the year 2000 is over.

In the coming years, we're going to see accountability become even more of a focus area, along with continued heavy focus on the security of data and customer privacy. We read a lot in the news about customer records that have been stolen or violated. A strong focus on reducing the total costs of technology ownership within the business will also occur. Technology is still one of the few areas in the company that can be perceived as an enabler of cost reduction. There will also be more focus on managing change in the business, and technology is going to become a bigger part of that process.

Steve Hannah has more than twenty-five years of technology, database, and leadership experience helping companies improve their return on their technology investment through the successful integration of information, technology, people, and process.

Currently serving as vice president and chief information officer for CRST International, he has been able to utilize his experience to define a vision for technology that is aligned with the objectives of the company and raise the bar on performance and service of the technology team.

Prior experience includes serving as vice president of technology with Knight Ridder, vice president of information technology for Gazette Communications, and computer services manager for Journal/Sentinel Inc.

Mr. Hannah earned his B.S. degree in computer science from Eastern Michigan University.